The ABCs of Classy

A Journey to Confidence, Self-Love and Transformation

Berthille Metoua

Published by Atlantique LLC

© 2026 Berthille Metoua
All rights reserved.
First edition. The ABCs of Classy

ISBN (paperback): 979-8-9941777-5-4
ISBN (Hardcover): 979-8-9941777-7-8
ISBN (eBook): 979-8-9941777-8-5

Author: Berthille Metoua
www.berthillemetoua.com
www.theabcsofclassy.com

About the Author

Berthille Metoua
Author · Speaker · Educator · Digital Designer

Berthille is a philanthropist and founder of AideHHC, dedicated to helping communities. Her work is shaped by experience in fashion and human services, authoring **1,000+ individualized life plans**.

Through her multicultural experience and education, Berthille translates complex ideas into practical, everyday steps—she created the Classy Check app, helping people present their best selves and boost confidence. She designs courses and resources in plain, accessible language. She lives by a simple belief: **learning is a lifelong journey. Education:** M.A. in Communications (Public Relations), **Southern New Hampshire University (SNHU)**; B.A. in Psychology, **Queens College**; and certificates in **Web Design**, **Database Management**, and **Business Management (Spanish American Institute)**.

Personal: Berthille Metoua was married to NST Cophie's, an Afro-disco musician and singer who passed away in 2020.

Connect & Updates

hello@berthillemetoua.com

berthillemetoua.com

Author's Quotes

"Discipline is a way to show self-love."
— Berthille Metoua

"Keep your face and hair neat—they greet the world before your words and set the first impression."
— Berthille Metoua

"Every change in life is an invitation to navigate with courage. Embrace what you have and find strengths you never knew you had."
— Berthille Metoua

"Most of what we say is beyond words."
— Berthille Metoua

Dear Reader,

I invite you to join me on a journey of refinement, growth, and self-discovery. This book is a reminder that each of us carries value—and that value can make a difference, not only in our own lives, but in the world around us.

Being classy is not about perfection—it is about intention, integrity, culture, discipline, and the way you carry yourself when no one is watching.

As you turn each page, take what speaks to you, reflect honestly, and apply it with consistency —small choices, repeated daily, create a powerful transformation.

Warmest Regards,

Berthille Metoua

CONTENTS

INTRODUCTION

How This Book Was Made and What **Inspired Me?** Writing this book has been one of the most unique experiences of my life. After graduating with my master's degree in 2016, I wrote it as part of my preparation for admission to a doctoral program. I told my educational story because it was full of challenges and pauses. As a gifted child and later a straight-A student, I once received an F grade and fell from academic excellence to academic probation— before working my way back to the honor roll. Still, I never gave up.

I questioned whether I should continue — especially when I could earn money in the modeling business with a high school diploma. During this period, I also learned to speak Hebrew, expanding my cultural and linguistic horizons. Yet, I realized my journey was worth sharing. I considered naming the book "Success Rather Than Education," but even that didn't feel quite right. I doubted whether my story would matter, thinking, "If you know so much, why aren't you rich yet?" So, I paused again.

Eventually, I wrote without worrying about the subject or title. That is how this book came to be— **The ABCs of Classy**. Through meditation and self-reflection, I discovered the truth about myself and my education— lessons learned through working in so many places. What once felt like setbacks turned out to be the best learning experiences of my life.

Everything I did in my career, from modeling and working as a waitress, moving into the fashion business and working as a real estate agent, to becoming a loan officer and PR specialist, then advancing to supervisor, and now a trainer and business owner—each role has taught me valuable lessons that I am excited to share. I grew up with two very intellectual and classy parents: my late father, a noble Deputy and owner of several businesses—including the biggest college in Abidjan in the 1970s—and my late mother, a forestry contractor and an esthetician's owner of multiple salon spas. Although this book isn't only about what I learned from them, they were my idols, my role models, and my greatest inspiration. They accomplished so much and are always remembered. They gave me the strength to pursue my education and career. My father used to take me to his school to teach when I was only twelve and would say, "You can do it." That was my first experience working as a teacher.

A pivotal moment in my life came when I became pregnant with my son. His birth became my inspiration to refocus on my goals and education, reminding me of the importance of perseverance and growth.

Guided by the lessons learned from my multicultural background, my parents' example, and my perseverance, I shaped this book, **"The ABCs of Classy,"** as a practical roadmap for anyone seeking growth, resilience, and style. Each chapter is a memorable lesson to learn, from A for Appropriateness to Z for Your Zone, reflecting a principle that helped navigate life's challenges and triumphs. I hope these stories and strategies will inspire you to embrace your own journey and pursue a truly classy life, one word at a time.

A FOR APPROPRIATENESS

Appropriateness is not just a virtue. It is a weapon of refinement. It's what you do around people — and the decisions you make. Let's make it real.

Someone slaps you in the face. That's inappropriate. If you fight back, is that inappropriate too? So, what do you do? You walk away immediately, get safe, and report it to the right person. That is not a weakness. That is control. That is how appropriate people operate.

Someone curses at you. If you curse back, is that also inappropriate?

Don't match their chaos. Don't give them your energy for free. Look them in the eyes and say, *"I can see you're upset. What do you need?"* — not because you are scared, but because you are trained. Because you refuse to be dragged.

Someone yells at you. Don't yell back to prove you have a voice. Lower yours. Slow down.

Ask one question that forces maturity into the room: *"What exactly are you feeling right now?"* That question is a mirror — and most people cannot handle their own reflection.

Fight back if someone hits you. Don't come home crying. And don't tell me the story unless you beat them.

Most mothers said it. And what they were really saying was not to be violent — it was to be unshakeable. To know yourself so well that nothing could pull you out of yourself.

And here is the one that separates the truly appropriate from the performative: if you dislike someone, you can still respect their effort. You can still say thank you when something is done right. *Appropriateness does not require you to be fake. It requires you to be fair — and capable of making strong decisions.*

There is always an appropriate way to respond. There is always a smarter way to disagree. There is always a cleaner way to express your feelings without diminishing yourself.

Appropriateness is discipline — inside and outside. It is how you show up.

And how you show up starts before you ever leave the house. It starts with one decision most people underestimate entirely — choosing your outfit.

It is the decision that carries you through the entire day — affecting your posture, your mood, your confidence, and the way people receive you before you say one word.

Successful people wouldn't build systems around it if it didn't matter. Some hire a stylist. Some use an assistant. Some keep a signature look — a white shirt, a black outfit — every single day. Different methods. Same mindset: protect your morning energy.

Here is the truth most people don't want to hear. The average person spends **close to one hour every morning** deciding what to wear — changing outfits, searching for pieces, doubting the mirror, starting over. One hour. Every single day. That is five hours a week. Over twenty hours a month. Gone — not on work, not on family, not on growth. On confusion that could have been solved the night before.

And it is not just the time. It is the energy. It is the cost nobody calculates.

When you wake up, your battery (energy) is at 100%. Your mind is clearest. Your patience is strongest. Your decisions are sharpest. That is your full capacity — and it is the most valuable window of your entire day. But when you waste that window fighting your closet, you drain your battery before the day even begins. Then you spend the rest of the day trying to recover what you had at the very start.

Now let's make it real with an example.

Your Morning Power Window

My wake-up time: 6:00 AM

My leaving time: 8:00 AM

My total morning time: 120 minutes

Now subtract what you must do every morning:

Hygiene (shower, face care, teeth): 20 minutes

Grooming (hair, dressing, makeup, beard): 25 minutes

Breakfast, coffee, water: 30 minutes

Prayer or meditation: 15 minutes

Packing (keys, wallet, lunch bag): 10 minutes

Buffer for unexpected delays: 5 minutes

Total used: 105 minutes. Remaining: 15 minutes.

What remains is your most precious time. That number is your truth. That is the window where your real morning energy should go — not outfit panic, not searching for a missing shoe, not standing in front of a mirror unsure of yourself.

You can use these 15 minutes in a way that feels rewarding or sets a positive tone for the rest of your day. For instance, try gentle stretching, reading a few pages of a book, writing in a journal, taking a short walk, rehearsal for the day, or even a simple check-in with your calendar or to-do list can help you feel more prepared. Use this time to experiment with what leaves you feeling most energized and focused.

 This Morning Power Window schedule shows how the method works. Change the times to fit your own mornings and needs. To make it more personal, think about what matters most to you and adjust the order or timing of activities to match your priorities.

Most people discover their real morning window is far smaller than they imagined. Some have fifteen minutes. Some have five. Some have none — which means they have already been starting every day in debt.

Appropriate people do not decide in the morning. They execute a decision already made.

The night before: lay out your complete outfit — clothes, shoes, bag, accessories. One decision, made in peace, when you are not rushed.

Plan your week on Sunday: select all five outfits before the week begins. Hang them in order. Your mornings are now yours.

Build by occasion, not by quantity: organize your wardrobe by category — work, casual, formal, ready-to-go. You do not need more clothes. You need the right clothes in the right place.

Keep one go-to outfit always ready: polished, complete, zero thought required — for the unexpected invitation, the last-minute meeting, the moment that does not wait.

Sunday reset: five minutes to check what needs washing, ironing, or replacing. This prevents every Monday morning crisis.

By the time morning arrives, the decision is already made. You are not choosing — you are executing. That is the difference between someone who arrives prepared and someone who simply arrives.

So here is the real question: What do you choose to show up for? Because when you show up prepared, you do not just arrive on time. You arrive correctly.

Being appropriate boosts your personal life and improves your interaction with others. How we dress and conduct ourselves reveals our character and our respect for the people around us. This is about your style — what is acceptable, and what is not.[1] It involves dressing for different occasions, knowing when formal attire is required, and when casual elegance is the right call.

Dressing with attention to context sets the foundation for your image. In a world of evolving social norms, true class goes beyond appearances — it includes how you present yourself, behave, and communicate.[2]

Imagine opening your closet each morning and feeling calm instead of overwhelmed. A wardrobe organized around your actual life — your weekends, your work, your special moments. When everything fits your real routine, getting dressed becomes easy. Your closet is not a storage unit. It reflects who you are. [3]And if the process ever feels like too much, there is no shame in asking for help — a stylist, a trusted friend, or a simple reorganization can change everything.[4]

For casual gatherings, brunches, or weekend outings, aim for effortless and chic — comfort and style working together.[5] For business settings, your clothes speak before you do. When you choose the right outfit for a meeting, an interview, or a networking event, you send a message of confidence and respect.[6] Mastering business attire is not about following rules — it is about showing the world your attention to detail and your commitment to making a memorable impression.[7]

For formal events, elegance is non-negotiable. Build a small ready collection — go-to pieces for black-tie occasions and galas — so the perfect outfit is always at hand. [8]Whether you are new to style or a seasoned fashionista, the goal is always the same: walk into any room knowing you are dressed for it.[9]

Cultural awareness matters too. When you travel or engage with people from different countries, understanding their expectations around attire shows respect and builds genuine connection.[10] Dressing appropriately for a culture is not a constraint — it is a form of intelligence. It fosters trust before a single word is spoken.[11]

Nothing communicates appropriateness more powerfully than dressing for the occasion — whether you are a CEO, a professional, or someone building their way up. Understand dress codes, the significance of uniforms, and the difference between representing your role and hiding behind your clothes.[12,13]

Key takeaway: Aligning your attire with your setting makes a strong, lasting impact.[14]

Beyond attire, appropriateness is also about how you speak and the words you choose. Tone of voice commands attention and respect. When you dress with intention and communicate with purpose, you open doors — professionally and personally.[15]

As you move through the world and encounter different cultures, appropriateness becomes a form of cultural harmony. Respecting dress codes, learning local customs, and entering spaces with awareness are not small gestures. They are how class actually travels.[16]

Mastering the art of presence does not require surgery. Cosmetic procedures can be beneficial when chosen freely and wisely, but they are never a requirement for confidence or class. Research confirms that interest in cosmetic alteration is often driven by peer pressure, social comparison, and body dissatisfaction — not genuine self-improvement.[17] Your body represents who you are. People sense confidence in how you carry yourself. Make decisions that align with your values and feel right for you.

Appropriateness is not a rule. It is a standard you set for yourself — and then refuse to lower yourself to anyone.

B FOR BEAUTY

Beauty is the sum of your habits, your choices, and your confidence. Make it visible. Staying beautiful is essential; people are drawn to radiance, not dullness. Beauty attracts opportunities and is achieved with care, not perfection. Would you want to watch something ugly when you can watch something beautiful? If you can choose better, why choose less? Present yourself intentionally—details show self-respect.

It's easy to feel lost in the endless beauty aisles and swirling trends, but what truly matters is staying authentic to yourself. Choose products that genuinely work for you, not because they're in style. Take your time, trust your instincts, and tune out the outside noise—your beauty is unique. When you embrace what makes you different, you leave a lasting impression by being yourself.

True beauty isn't about fitting a mold—it's about letting your inner light shine through your face and hair. Walk into each day with quiet confidence, trusting that you look your best when you're yourself. The most genuine beauty unfolds as you discover and empower who you are. Let your face and hair reflect your personality and spirit— *Keep your face and hair neat—they greet the world before your words and set the first impression.* They're what people notice first, and they tell your story before you even speak.

This lesson reminds me of Nathalie, a young woman navigating the challenges of modern life while aspiring to embrace true elegance. At 5'6", with short, faded hair and little confidence, Nathalie began her journey much like many of us: unsure, but hopeful. When she joined my agency, I guided her transformation step by step—posture, nails, skincare, hair, and wardrobe. She approached each stage with openness and determination. But her most important transformation wasn't about products or routines; it was about discovering her inner strength. Over time, Nathalie realized that genuine beauty starts from within. As she embraced her true self, she blossomed—radiating confidence and a glow that can't be bought. Research also suggests that makeup can influence self-perception, confidence, and social interaction[18].

Prioritize your face and hair. Get professional help when needed: a licensed hairstylist, a makeup lesson, or learn the techniques yourself.

When it comes to procedures, remember that you can achieve brilliance without cosmetic surgery. When considering any procedure, research the risks, choose accredited providers, and prioritize your health over fleeting trends. Make your decisions based on your well-being, not on media or external pressures. Trends come and go, but your health endures.

Hands and nails: the quiet tell.

Clean, neat nails are the finishing touch. If you prefer nail polish that lasts, wear gel polish. Keep them tidy between appointments. If you can't maintain length, keep them short and clean.[19]

Good grooming whispers credibility. There is a certain satisfaction that comes from having clean, well-done nails. It's like the finishing touch to a masterpiece. A signal to the world that you pay attention to the details. Since appearances matter, neglecting your nails is like leaving dust in a freshly cleaned house. The importance of keeping your nails clean and well-maintained is a crucial aspect of personal grooming that should not be overlooked.

The perfect outfit, makeup, and hair can't hide messy nails—they stand out like a blemish. Clean neat nails show attention to detail and hygiene. Neglecting them can suggest that something more profound is wrong.[20]

Think how much unseen dirt exists. Some people wonder why they weren't called back after a date—dirty nails might be the reason. If you can't care for your nails, keep them short.

Imagine a royal family member with a very long nail—how odd! With today's nail polish options, there's no excuse to neglect this part of grooming. The right polish can elevate your style.

Your nails say a lot about you. This small detail can significantly impact how others perceive you. Whether you're busy or fashion-forward, keeping nails clean and neat shows self-care and respect. Pay attention to details—they matter.

Maintaining clean nails isn't vanity—it's presenting your best self. Shaking hands with someone whose nails are dirty leaves a poor impression. People with well-cared-for hands typically feel confident using hand gestures and aren't embarrassed to extend their hands for handshakes.[21]

Learn how to apply nails and makeup and select the right makeup. Start by learning which type of face you have: triangular, oval, square, long, or circular? Your makeup is your primary tool for facial appearance. For this reason, it is essential to know how to apply makeup to your face type, as there are different techniques for each.[22]

Ms. Metoua (Berthille's Mother)

Your face is your first sign of beauty. Beauty can require a big budget, but that wasn't true for my mother, an esthetician and beauty specialist—who taught me, "You can always stay beautiful even with a small budget." She was the most beautiful woman I've seen. She also shared this beauty secret.

<u>Classy Beauty Recipes (always patch test first and check with your dermatologist).</u>

Warm Egg Massage

Hard-boil an egg; peel while hot; wrap in clean linen.

Roll in gentle circles over the forehead, eyes (closed), nose, lips, chin, and neck.

Wipe off residue with a cotton cloth, rinse with warm water. Repeat every 2 weeks.

Flour Mask (nourish/soften)

½ glass of milk warmed + 1 tbsp honey.

Stir in 4–5 tablespoons of fresh wheat/oat/buckwheat flour.

Add 1 tbsp of olive oil and a squeeze of lemon juice. Warm gently (Bain-marie).

Apply for 20 minutes, rinse with warm water.

Carrot + Parsley Mask (brightening)

Blend carrot and parsley.

Apply a thick layer to the face/neck for 20 minutes, rinse with warm water.

Helps clarity, smoothness, and suppleness.

Hydration helps your glow. Our bodies are composed of approximately 60% water, and hydration plays a vital role in supporting overall health and the appearance of our skin.[23] Proper hydration is associated with healthier aging.[24] Water first; beauty follows.

Makeup guardrails that keep you polished:

Avoid heavy daytime foundation—it magnifies texture.

Avoid shades that are too dark or too light for your neck.

Blend blush softly; skip harsh "doll" patches.

Use smoky eyes thoughtfully; harsh versions can make the eyes appear older.

Don't layer dark powder over a lighter base.

Skip greasy/powdery creams that cake.

No powder on freshly tanned skin.

Apply lipstick with a mirror/brush—especially with fine lines.

Light can deceive; use daylight during the day and look for warm artificial light in the evening.

The best makeup looks like great skin, not great makeup.

Everyday principles to keep you timeless:

Wear makeup when you go out if it helps you feel prepared and polished.

Keep your routine realistic: cleanse, treat, and moisturize; protect your hair from heat.

Schedule periodic professional check-ins (haircut, brow shaping, skin consultation).

Learn continuously—but only keep what serves you.

Elegance is a routine you can repeat.

Closing reminders: Don't chase every product; curate your habits. Confidence, cleanliness, and care are the most powerful beauty secrets.

Main takeaway: These three qualities underpin all other beauty efforts.

Beauty Must-Haves Checklist

Cleanser (gentle; for your skin type)

Makeup remover (micellar, oil, balm, or cream)

Serum (one targeted need: vitamin C, niacinamide, hyaluronic acid, or retinol—choose what suits you)

Moisturizer (day and/or night, as needed)

Foundation or skin tint (True Match shade)

Concealer (target areas only)

Setting option (sheer powder or spray—light touch)

Blush or bronzer (soft, buildable)

Brow groomer (pencil/gel to frame the face)

Mascara (clean formula you tolerate)

Lip liner + balm/lipstick/natural gloss

Beauty sponge/brush set (keep clean)

Thermal water/Evian Brumisateur (optional refresh)

Weekly mask (clarify, hydrate, or soothe)

Hair basics (clarifying + hydrating wash; heat protectant)

Tools: tweezers, lash curler, clothing steamer (for a polished presentation)

Your true beauty comes from embracing your individuality. Ignore outside noise and focus on what suits you. Listen to your face and hair, and choose treatments aligned with your essence. Authenticity is your most powerful beauty secret.

If you decide to get facial surgery, a Brazilian butt lift, butt injection augmentation, or silicone butt injection. First, check for potential side effects and complications based on your health. Although I do not suggest that anyone undergo surgery, some people may need to do so, regardless of any beauty tips. If you feel uncertain about your beauty to that point, research the risks of the procedures and ensure that they are performed in a hospital or an accredited surgery center. Perhaps search for stories of surgical disasters and botches to prepare yourself for the worst. Remember that Meghan did not undergo surgery for Prince Harry to choose her—this is an excellent example of the power of confidence and the unimportance of surgical alterations.[25] The fact is, you will attract the right person if you put in the work. True beauty is not a one-size-fits-all concept. It's a reflection of your inner radiance exuding through your face and hair. So, go forth with confidence, knowing that you look best when you stay true to yourself. Beauty untangled awaits you on your journey to self-discovery and empowerment. May your face and hair always reflect the beauty within.

Beauty is the reflection of our ancestry. We remember the beauty of those who came before us, and their image reminds us to stay beautiful. I remember my mother as a beautiful soul; I'm inspired to carry that beauty forward in myself. Let the beauty of your ancestry inspire you to cherish and celebrate your own.

C FOR CLASSY

Classy is simple. It is a mindset rooted in authenticity, grace, and thoughtfulness. It is about understanding your worth and acting in ways that honor it. True class comes from knowing yourself and living in alignment with that self-knowledge, rather than material wealth.

What Does It Mean to Be Classy?

Being classy means acting with authenticity and grace in both private and public life. It is defined by how you treat others and face challenges—always choosing integrity and self-respect.

Classy Woman: Carry your handbag on the left side. Keep your right hand free for introductions and handshakes. When walking with a partner, hold his arm with your right hand.

Classy Man: Traditionally, a gentleman offers his left arm and keeps his right hand free—

ready to guide, assist, and protect if necessary. Adjust as needed for the setting.

Classy Tips for Everyone:

Take care to be clean, practice good hygiene, and maintain a pleasant scent.

Emotional Intelligence

Always aim to smell pleasant as part of your routine.

Dress suitably for all occasions, reflecting personal style and context.

Show respect to everyone and offer to help others.

Don't depend on brand names to look good— know how to dress well regardless of labels.

Be financially responsible, confident, and comfortable.

Engage in physical activity, and if possible, try taking part in multiple sports.

Take an active role in your professional and personal development.

Avoid tattoos or keep them minimal and discreet if you must have them.

Keep your nails neat, clean, and groomed, if that aligns with your preferences.

Dress appropriately for each occasion, balancing elegance and appropriateness.

Minimize your makeup and opt for a natural, elegant look if you choose to wear it.

Maintain a mindset of learning.

Maintain composure and moderate your drinking if you choose to do so.

Consider choosing classic accessories, such as pearls. Pearls are timeless, always fashionable, and often passed down as heirlooms. Each pearl represents strength and quiet elegance. [26]

A Classy Mind & Classy Attitude

Class starts with self-respect, curiosity, and a commitment to growth. A classy person consistently makes good choices, builds positive habits, and treats others with dignity. The essence of class is seen in authentic thought and action, poise, and kindness. Confidence, punctuality, and striving to be your best self define the classy mindset.

Living Classy on a Budget

Choose quality over quantity.

Select affordable, well-made accessories.

Prepare your own meals and beauty treatments.

Focus on self-respect, kindness, and continuous learning.

The Classy Musts

Know how to tie a tie.

Know how to set a table.

Know how to open a bottle of wine or champagne with confidence.

Sew, iron, and dress appropriately for every situation.

Introduce yourself well and conduct yourself with dignity.

Show respect to everyone you meet.

Behave with grace at the table and learn to cook.

Exercise regularly and participate in at least one sport.

Join a community and be punctual.

Give generously.

Remember essential dates and keep your agenda updated.

Maintain good hygiene and a pleasant scent.

Keep a strong circle of support.

Take care of your appearance.

 Never display brand names unless you're being paid to do so.

Attend interesting events.

Understand body language.

Stay informed about key people in your field.

Keep up with the news, including financial and stock updates.

Know the meaning of important gifts, including roses.

The dining table is where your manners are most visible and others most often judge you. You might dress well, speak clearly, and act with confidence, but all of that can be undone if you do not know which bread plate is yours or how to get a waiter's attention politely. These small details separate someone who knows about elegance from someone who truly lives it. *We reveal who we are at the table. It is not just where we eat.*

The Place Setting: Know What Is in Front of You. Before the meal begins, orient yourself. The rule is simple: all drinks—glasses, cups, wine—are on your right. All solid items—bread plate and salad—are on your left. Your forks sit on the left, knives and spoons on the right. Use utensils from the outside in as each course arrives.

Your bread plate is always to your left.[27] Remember: BMW. Bread, Meal, Water — left to right. If you are ever unsure which bread plate or glass is yours, this three-word sequence will save you every time. Note: the BMW refers to your water glass which sits above the knife on the right— a reminder that all drinks are on that side.

The Napkin — Communicating for You

As soon as you are seated, place your napkin across your lap, folded in half with the fold facing you.[28] If you must leave the table during the meal, place the napkin loosely on your chair — not on the table. When the meal is complete, leave the napkin loosely folded to the left of your plate.[29] A neatly folded napkin at the end of a meal signals to the server that you were unhappy. Leave it naturally placed.

How to Signal Your Waiter?

You do not wave, snap, or call out across the room.[30] You make eye contact. When your server is within a reasonable distance, you catch their eye and give a small, deliberate nod. That is sufficient. During dining, everything should be done quietly and with minimal disruption to those around you.

When You Do Not Recognize the Menu

Ask your server, "What would you recommend for someone who enjoys lighter flavors?" or "What is the kitchen proudest of tonight?"[31] Servers are trained to guide you, and a well-asked question will often result in the best dish in the house. Never order at random simply to seem confident. Curiosity is always more elegant than pretending.

Bread, Soup, and Salad — The Rules Most People Get Wrong.

Bread: Break it — do not cut it.[32] Tear a small piece, butter only that piece, and eat it. You do not butter the entire roll at once. The bread knife is for spreading, not cutting.

Soup: Spoon away from you, not toward you.[33] Sip quietly from the side of the spoon, never slurp. When the bowl is nearly empty, tip it slightly away from you to gather the last of it. Rest the spoon in the bowl when you are done — not on the saucer unless specifically provided.

Salad: If the lettuce pieces are large, cut them with your fork and knife rather than folding a large leaf into your mouth.[34] At a formal dinner, use the salad fork — the smaller one on the outside left.

Handling the Check — Who Pays? when? and how?

If you issued the invitation, you pay. This is non-negotiable. Inviting someone to dinner is implicitly offering to host, and hosting includes the check. If the invitation was mutual, the check conversation happens before the bill arrives — not as a scramble when it lands on the table.

If someone insists on paying when you invited them, accept gracefully the first time they offer, and if they insist a second time, allow it

— then make a point of hosting them again.[35] A classy person never argues over the check (loudly in a restaurant). The exchange is handled quickly, and without drama.

Conversation at the Table — What a Classy Person Never Discusses?

A formal dinner is not the place for: the cost of anything, medical details, relationship problems, contentious politics or religion with people you do not know well, complaints about the food, or your phone.[36] The phone should be out of sight unless there is a genuine emergency — and even then, you excuse yourself from the table before looking at it.[37]

What you do discuss: your genuine interest in the people around you. The most memorable dinner guest is never the one who talked the most — it is the one who made everyone else feel most interesting.[38]

Toasting — How to Do It Correctly?

When a toast is offered, raise your glass and make eye contact with the person being toasted — not with everyone around the table.[39] You do not drink to yourself if you are the one being honored. Hold your glass by the stem if it is a wine glass, to avoid warming the wine with your hand.[40] You do not clink glasses at a large formal table — that tradition is reserved for intimate settings.

Excusing Yourself from the Table

You wait for a natural pause in the conversation. You place your napkin on your chair. You say simply, "Excuse me for a moment," without explanation.[41] You do not announce where you are going. You return promptly and re-enter the conversation quietly, without drawing attention to your return.

 What a Classy Person Never Does at a Restaurant

Stack plates or try to help the waiter clear — that is their role.

Season food before tasting it — it implies the kitchen did not do its job.

Speak with food in their mouth.

Apply makeup, fix hair, or use a mirror at the table.

Complain about the wait, the service, or the food loudly enough for neighboring tables to hear.

Take food from someone else's plate without asking.

Scroll through their phone while others are speaking.

Order the most expensive item on the menu when someone else is paying.

Leave without acknowledging the host or saying a proper goodbye.

Ask for a doggy bag at a formal dinner.

Fragrance Essentials: What a Classy person need to know

Don't confuse "Eau de cologne", "Eau de toilette", "Eau de parfum", and "Parfum"—the aromatic compounds are different. Check the label for instructions on choosing and using the right fragrance.[42] Use the right tools for every task. Match your clothing colors correctly.

Changing your perfume with the seasons isn't a trend—it's also about how fragrance behaves in different weather. In warm temperatures, scent molecules evaporate and diffuse more quickly, which can make a perfume feel stronger at first but fade faster. In colder weather, evaporation slows down, so lighter notes may feel quieter while deeper, richer notes can feel smoother and longer lasting.[43] That's why many people prefer brighter, airy scents in summer and warmer, heavier scents in fall and winter.

There's also a psychological side to it. Smell is closely linked to emotion and memory, so certain notes can feel "right" at different times of year because they match our mood, routines, and seasonal memories.[44] When choosing a seasonal fragrance, think about how the climate will affect performance, what you want to feel (energy, comfort, confidence), and which scents connect you to positive experiences from that season.

D FOR DANCE

Dance is about letting go, shaking off stress, or allowing music to move you. Dance is the hidden language of the soul.45 To dance is to be out of yourself-larger, more beautiful, more powerful. 46Learning to dance is more than memorizing steps—it's a way to express who you are with grace and confidence. Each step, even if you don't think of yourself as a dancer, is a chance to tell your own story. The moment you step onto the dance floor, the pulse of the bass vibrating through the music— something magical happens. You don't have to do too much or aim for perfection; move with intention and let your personality shine through every motion.

During primary school, my parents enrolled me in classical dance. I was a ballet dancer until I was ten years old. I can still recall the first time I executed a plié at the barre; my muscles tight yet determined to bend with grace. Each arabesque left a subtle ache but instilled in me a poise that felt like a secret language of elegance. When my family moved to a new borough, the school had no dance classes, so I stopped taking them. Classical dance taught me elegance and poise, and it is my foundation—where I learned to embody femininity. I suggest that every woman try classical dance at least once. 47

Later, as a teenager, I found myself drawn to a high school group that was all about rock 'n' roll dancing—it was in vogue back then. I quickly fell in love with it, throwing myself into every practice and even starting to compete. Nights out with friends became chances to express myself, not a routine. Dance has been my steady companion throughout these years, bringing bursts of joy and meaning to my life. Becoming a certified Zumba instructor opened even more ways to move and connect with others. But no matter what style I try, the influence of my classical roots gives my dancing a certain grace and discipline, no matter where the music takes me.

The power of dance is to let music move you and express your true self. One memorable influence for me is Janet Jackson's "The Pleasure Principle" (1986)—I danced to it, and its energy and sense of freedom stand out in my memories.

Dance movies do more than entertain—they inspire us to move, believe in transformation, and create connection. Films like "Flashdance"

(1983), "Save the Last Dance" (2001), "Step Up" (2006) & Step Up 2:The Streets (2008), "Stomp the Yard" (2007), John Travolta's "Saturday Night Fever" (1977), and Patrick Swayze's "Dirty Dancing" (1987) have motivated audiences to embrace the magic of dance.48

Why is it so important to learn how to dance? The answer is not in mastering flashy moves, but in building the confidence to own your space and move with elegance. At parties, many feel self-conscious when others glide effortlessly across the floor, but dancing is about finding your rhythm, connecting, expressing, and letting go. Sincerity matters more than complex moves. Whether your style is classic, hip-hop, rock 'n' roll, salsa, belly dancing, or Afro-beat, you don't need to be a professional. Learn a few moves so you can enjoy any event without embarrassment. Dancing reveals personality—you get to know people by seeing them have fun on the dance floor.49

Dance and music are inseparable—music is the heartbeat that gives meaning to movement. None of these experiences stand alone. Music's wide variety can be overwhelming, but it shapes our moods, memories, and well-being.

Music affects our bodies and minds by carrying energetic frequencies that influence how we feel and move. Some songs aid healing and relaxation, like those tuned to 432 Hz, while others, such as those tuned to 528 Hz, are said to enhance love and harmony. Certain tracks can foster confidence, imagination (963 Hz), or spiritual awakening (111 Hz). Very low-frequency bass makes people want to move—research shows that when music includes this, people dance nearly 12 percent more, often driven by sounds we don't consciously notice.50

Be selective with your music—what you listen to affects healing, relaxation, and overall well-being. Teach children this mindfulness as well. Our well-being depends on informed music choices. Research shows that music affects our physical movement, emotions, and overall well-being."51

Natural sounds—like birds, water, and forests—are powerful aids for relaxation and quality sleep. Listening to them at night can help you rest and enjoy each moment.52

Experts also explore the connection between music and the human body. For instance, Michel Gautier's TEDx talk explores the connection between music and the human body. He says we have seven energy centers, each tied to a musical note (Do, Re, Mi, Fa, Sol, La, Si), and each organ resonates at its own frequency. Even amino acids vibrate at specific frequencies. Gautier highlights Pachelbel's "Canon in D"—listening to it daily can nourish us and reduce stress. Our bodies need eight amino acids, and this piece supports those needs energetically. If stressed, listen to "Canon in D" to restore balance.53

The joy and authenticity found in dance and music matter far more than perfection. What's most important is to enjoy the moment, let your personality shine, and embrace the transformation power of moving and listening with confidence.

E FOR EDUCATION

Education isn't a diploma hanging on the wall or a degree listed on a resume. It's a lifelong adventure—sometimes messy, often surprising, and always full of growth. When you learn something new, you unlearn things you thought you knew, and sometimes you look back and laugh at how far you've come. Sure, lots of people think education is about collecting certificates or acing exams, but it's so much deeper than that. Proper education is found in those small, everyday moments—figuring out a new recipe, asking questions at work, or having a heart-to-heart with a friend. It's the curiosity that nudges you to try, fail, and try again. Inside the classroom or out in the world, every lesson counts, and it's this ongoing openness to learning that truly shapes who you become.

Being classy means pursuing education or mastering a skill that uses your unique talent while demonstrating elegance, respect for others, good manners, and sophistication.[54]

However, class is not a fixed trait; it is a mindset that can be cultivated and developed over time.[55] Through deliberate practice and a commitment to personal growth, anyone can learn to embody these qualities. There are countless learning opportunities, from online classes and webcasts to technical schools. According to the Career Technical Education Facilities Program, the State Allocation Board has approved $300 million for the next CTEFP funding cycle, supporting learning opportunities at various levels. People continue to learn every day, whether through intentional effort or through daily experiences.[56] Choose what you want to learn so you're not overwhelmed with any type of published information but focus on your preferred career or interest.

However, formal education is not the only path to success. According to a CNBC report, several occupations offer six-figure salaries without a college degree.[57] What matters is your dedication, your talent, and your openness to learning new things. These qualities are the key to opening doors for anyone. Take barbers, for instance. They excel through continuous improvement, honing their skills to perfection. Hairdressers show proactive service, always staying ahead with trends to offer clients the latest styles.[58] Singers rely on relentless practice to perfect their craft. Designers embrace creativity and adapt to ever-changing aesthetics.

Success is attainable beyond traditional educational paths. According to Greenhow and Lewin, education now extends beyond traditional classroom boundaries, and social media can help bridge formal and informal learning by supporting the development of various talents and skills.[59] While diplomas or higher education can open career doors, true education encompasses much more.

Showing respect to others and earning their respect remain key to social harmony. Imagine walking into a cozy café, where the scent of freshly brewed coffee fills the air. You approach the counter, and a barista greets you with a bright smile and a warm 'Good morning! How can I help you today?' Such gestures, although simple, convey a deep understanding of respect in human interactions. It's in these small but meaningful acts, along with using proper etiquette, where we truly show respect. We'll return to this in the chapter on knowledge. For now, the next two paragraphs lay out the distinction.

Education is valuable, but knowledge gained through life experience can be as powerful. Think of education as a map that provides direction and structure, while the knowledge gained through experience is the journey that fills in the details, bringing the map to life. Education is acquired typically through formal study at schools and universities, while knowledge is often gained through personal growth and life experiences. Both are valuable, and together they shape who we become.

Knowledge is the process by which skills and expertise are passed from one generation to the next through teaching, training, or research. Any experience shaping your thinking, feelings, or actions is educational. Education is typically structured into distinct stages, including preschool, primary school, secondary school, college, university, and apprenticeships.[60] Education typically occurs with teacher guidance, but knowledge often comes informally through practice and dedication, passed down. [61]

Today, we benefit from formal education thanks to international agreements and laws, but practical knowledge is still gained through experience and personal growth. Before I share my story, take a moment to reflect on your own learning experiences. Who were your first teachers? What values and lessons did your home environment emphasize? My understanding of what it means to be classy, which includes showing elegance, refined manners, and respect for others, began at home. My parents were my most excellent teachers, instilling in me the values of a classy lifestyle through their elegant living, strict rules, and encouragement to read books and magazines, as well as to pursue my education. I learned the importance of manners, presentation, and discipline long before I ever entered formal schooling.

As I grew, my education expanded beyond the classroom. Managing a modeling agency and traveling exposed me to different cultures and deepened my appreciation for elegance. The National Geographic report notes that although travel can shape our minds, achieving genuine empathy is more complex and not automatically guaranteed by these experiences. Running a brand-name store honed my management skills; while working as a habitation counselor and CASAC-T (Credentialed Alcohol and Substance Abuse Counselor Training) developed my behavioral insight for handling challenging situations. Supporting teens in foster care and people with psychiatric illness taught me lessons no textbook offers, particularly in developing a deep sense of empathy. Creating thousands of life plans as a QIDP (Qualified Intellectual Disability Professional) enhanced my capacity for detailed planning and a personalized approach. These roles cultivated valuable skills that transcended their contexts, offering a broader perspective and deeper understanding in my professional journey.

My journey didn't stop with formal education. Work in real estate, event organization, and other roles all shaped my understanding of class, hospitality, and etiquette. These experiences taught me real-world lessons no classroom could provide. Training others has become my most significant source of fulfillment, letting me both share knowledge and continue learning myself.

Of course, formal education mattered too. According to a study by Asefeh Asemi and Elham Aghajan, earning a master's degree can impact graduates in various ways, including improving essential skills such as writing, research, and critical thinking. In my journey toward education, my father (pictured below) was my symbol of learning and my motivation to complete my graduation. Sometimes, without motivation, it is hard to go through this journey. For that reason, choose one symbol for yourself, set a clear goal, and attach a source of inspiration to it. Every element of this journey can lead you closer to your education goals—and to any other goals you choose to pursue.

Berthille Metoua and her Father Mr. Metoua

The most considerable growth occurred from combining education and experience, both domestically and globally. Research shows that while social media can be used for academic purposes, it is often more of a distraction and impacts academic performance, especially among first-year students. Nearly every platform can serve as a search engine for information, making it a valuable resource for finding relevant content.62 However, it's important to check the reliability of sources and the background of those sharing information. There's nothing worse than learning the wrong thing, as it's much harder to unlearn misinformation.63 Another challenge with social media learning is the brevity of content. You might only get a highlight from a minute video, leaving much more to learn.

To turn caution into a practical skill, let's explore a simple fact-checking process you can apply to claims and quotes you encounter online. Imagine you come across a TikTok video with health tips. First, examine the creator's profile to check their credentials. Look for any links to professional websites or credentials in the health field. If such links exist, try verifying their details by cross-referencing them with reputable sources, such as health organization websites. Review the video's comments to see if they offer insights or corrections from professionals. If possible, find similar content from trusted sources to compare the information.

Moving across all social media: YouTube, Facebook, Instagram, X (formerly Twitter). Make sure you go through the same process before you share or practice. Some creators share information without proper sourcing, while others spread misinformation to gain views and likes. The process again is to check the publisher's credentials and background, then check the information resources. Whenever you are interested in learning, try to find a more extended version with clear resources.

Consider seeking books or professional resources for a better learning experience and understanding. Always remember, much of what you see online attracts and entertains, not to educate. For a more comprehensive learning experience, seek longer videos, follow professionals in your field, and use their advice to truly educate yourself.

F FOR FASHION

Fashion is about looking good with style, while Class is about choosing pieces intentionally. Quality over quantity plays a big role. Valuable clothes and jewelry that last reflect a mindset of respect for craftsmanship and sustainability. These pieces don't go out of style. For example, my mother gave me a black dress when I was a teenager, and I still have it; it never went out of style. That dress represents thoughtful choices and timeless elegance- not just ownership but beautiful and value. I felt the same way I did when I wore it for the first time. Now it's in my classy collection. This black dress is a testament to the timeless nature of certain pieces and the importance of investing in high-quality staples. While it's important to treasure these lasting pieces, it's also good to keep up with new designer collections. Knowing which designers fit your work wardrobe and which are best for special events makes a big difference. [64]

Fashion shows are a great way to see the latest trends and styles. For a memorable experience, try reaching out to your favorite designers for invitations. Attending different shows lets you enjoy the creativity and elegance of high fashion.

Designers are happy to share their newest styles with you. Try to update your wardrobe each season. Staying stylish means knowing when it's time for a change. When you shop, think about upcoming occasions like birthdays, holidays, and special events. Make sure you shop for each season.

Also, plan your shopping ahead of time for special occasions so you're ready for last-minute nights out, keeping your social plans and personal taste in mind. Stick to your style, but don't promote a brand unless you're being paid to do so.

Being consistent with my fashion choices has been a talent. I've discovered my style, and I believe it can work for anyone. People often remember you by how you present yourself, and that first impression sticks. According to Claire Butler, research shows that the clothes we choose to wear can directly affect our mood, thoughts, and behavior, a concept known as "enclothed cognition". This means that our outward style not only influences how others perceive us but also shapes how we feel about ourselves. That's why I think it's essential for all of us to be mindful not only of what we wear but also of our everyday choices—what we eat, what we read or watch, and the conversations we have. These details add up to the image we put out into the world. I encourage you to picture the best version of yourself and make daily choices that help you become that person.

Not every trend works for everyone. Dress in a way that fits your body, your style, and the occasion. This is where "F" for Fashion connects with Frequency: great style isn't random —it's the consistent practice of choosing what fits your body, your values, and occasion. By being consistent, you become what you project. Start each day by setting a morning style intention. As you get ready, choose an outfit that aligns with how you want to feel and how you want to present yourself throughout the day. According to *Psychology Today*, style involves making choices that reflect how you see yourself,[65] so it's essential to be mindful of the images and influences you surround yourself with, such as movies, friends, and even colors. Focus on the image you want to show, and choose what matches the person you want to be. If you're thinking about dressing for your age, remember: if an outfit is elegant and fits well, it works for any woman.[66] Skip the worst trends and always aim to look stylish.

For perfect color matches, consider using these simple pairings: Blue goes well with pink (think warm weather), yellow (autumn leaves), orange (complementary on the color wheel), black, white, and green. "BBRGOWG" is the mnemonic for these blue pairings. The red pairs beautifully with gold (royalty and luxury), beige (subtle and classic), brown, yellow (warmth and vibrancy), and pink. Beige can be worn seamlessly with brown, green (earthy tones), red, yellow, and black. Green suits blue, brown, yellow (spring freshness), and chocolate brown (rich and comforting). Gray matches well with red, black, or white. Black and white are universal anchors that match with any color, creating a classic palette. Remember: never mix one patterned piece with another. Patterns should complement plain-colored clothing to maintain a polished look [67] Any classy person should have a verification method— a quick way to double-check your look before stepping out is to use the new Classy Check app (ClassyCheck.com).

As we advance, match your shoes and bag to avoid a fashion mistake. According to NDTV Shopping, mixing textures like pairing a suede tote with matte-finish boots or matching metallic shoes with a clutch that has metallic accents can be an effective approach to coordinating your shoes and bag. If you find this challenging, you can also focus on ensuring your shoes complement your outfit. A black or brown bag works with almost any outfit, which is helpful if you're on a budget.[68] It's good to have a black and a brown bag, plus one in your favorite color. If you can, get a bag for every color you wear. For special occasions, make sure your accessories—bags, shoes, and jewelry—are perfectly matched to finish your look. To cater to different budgets, consider a "good-better-best" approach when selecting bags. Start with accessible brands like Target or H&M for budget-friendly options. As you move up, mid-range brands such as Fossil and Coach offer quality at reasonable prices. For a more luxurious touch, consider investing in premium brands like Michael Kors or Kate Spade that offer both style and longevity.

Common Style Types (for Men and Women):

Classic and elegant style: Timeless, polished looks build on refined tailoring and neutral colors. For men, think suits, blazers, and crisp shirts. For women, opt for tailored dresses, blouses, and structured pieces.

Artistic and vintage style: Unique, creative outfits with retro or handcrafted touches. Both men and women can express this with vintage finds, bold prints, or artistic accessories.

Edgy and dramatic style: Bold choices, statement pieces, and a willingness to stand out. This might include leather jackets, striking colors, or unexpected silhouettes for any gender.

Casual, relaxed style: Effortless, comfortable clothes like jeans, t-shirts, and soft fabrics. It's a favorite for anyone who values comfort and simplicity.

Romantic and feminine style: This style uses soft, flowing shapes, delicate details, and gentle colors. While it's usually linked to women, men can add romantic touches with softer fabrics, pastel colors, or vintage-inspired pieces.

Before you dive into these questions, take a moment to envision your ideal future self. Consider what aspects of your life you wish to enhance through your personal style and how you want others to perceive you. This reflection can help you provide more authentic responses.

Nine Questions to Help Define Your Personal Style

How familiar are you with your own style preferences and the way you want to present yourself?

Your stylist should understand you, not impose their own vision. Your style should reflect who you are, not someone else's idea of you.

Which colors do you naturally gravitate toward and enjoy wearing?

This can help you build a wardrobe that feels authentic and energizing.

What type of clothing makes you feel most confident and true to yourself?

Focus on what empowers you, whether it's sharp tailoring, relaxed fits, or bold statements.

What fabrics do you prefer for your everyday wardrobe?

Think about what feels best on your skin and fits your lifestyle, like cotton, wool, silk, or denim.

How do you like your clothes to fit? Do you prefer relaxed, tailored, or something in between?

Fit is personal and can completely change how you feel in your clothes.

Are there particular outfits or looks that boost your mood or give you energy?

Think about what you wear when you want to feel your best.

Which brands or designers align with your taste and values?

Look for labels that reflect your approach to fashion, whether that's sustainability, luxury, or timeless classics.

Who are your style icons or public figures you admire (male or female)?

Drawing inspiration from people you admire can help clarify your own style.

What activities or settings do you need your wardrobe to support (work, events, travel, etc.)?

Your style should fit your lifestyle, not the other way around.

Remember: Style is for everyone. The key is to make each style fit your personality and preferences, regardless of gender.

G FOR GLAMOUR

Glamour, an addition to fashion, enters the world of charm, allure, and the unforgettable impression one person can leave on another. Its core, glamour is audacious self-authenticity, a daring embrace of individuality that lets your true self shine through. It's about having a sense of creativity that flourishes once you develop a keen eye for fashion. Breaking conventional fashion rules becomes effortless when your charisma and memorable style captivate everyone around you. *Let your fashion choices speak for you, telling a story that is both unique and undeniable.*

Glamour starts with good grooming and keeping makeup light to highlight your natural beauty. Taking care of your skin and appearance is key to looking glamorous. Many people think glamour means being flashy, but it's about paying *attention to every detail, starting with your hair. Hair is often the first thing people notice, so keep it neat and styled, even when you sleep. Keeping your style coordinated helps you look*

your best and leaves a powerful impression.
Remember, practice makes perfect, so keep
working on your look to master glamour.

I didn't realize how many black outfits I had
until my mother pointed it out. When I
checked my closet, she was right. The colors
you wear each day matter. Wearing black all
the time can feel gloomy, so it's better to mix
in brighter colors. Think of Queen Elizabeth
II, who wore a different color every day. Her
style was about feeling vibrant and special, not
just glamorous. She also showed her style with
her choice of handbag, making her look
unique and elegant. This shows you don't have
to be flashy to make a lasting impression.

To bring the color of communication to life,
consider an experiment. Choose an upcoming
event, perhaps a presentation or a social
gathering, and select your outfit based on the
psychological effect you wish to achieve. For
example, wear blue to project calm and
trustworthiness, or red to display confidence
and passion. Observe others' reactions and
your own feelings throughout the event. This
practical application lets you test color
psychology firsthand, turning theory into a
personal experience.

Red screams confidence and passion-perfect
for a big presentation or a hot date. Spiritually,
red is linked to energy, action, and courage.

Blue is a calming and trustworthy color, perfect for conveying credibility and seriousness in interviews. Spiritually, blue represents peace, healing, and wisdom.

Yellow is often associated with energy, innovation, and a creative boost in your outfit, while spiritually it represents joy, clarity, and enlightenment. According to The New Yorker, Queen Elizabeth II was known for saying, "I have to be seen to be believed."

Green signals growth and balance, making it ideal for networking and forming new connections. Spiritually, green is about renewal, harmony, and prosperity.

Wearing purple says luxury and ambition; think big, dream bigger. Spiritually, purple is associated with intuition, royalty, and awareness.

Orange radiates friendliness and enthusiasm, great for social events and meeting new people. Spiritually, orange brings optimism, creativity, and emotional balance.

White is pure, and perfect for new beginnings. Spiritually, white means purity, protection, and spiritual awakening.

Black is powerful, sophisticated, and timeless. Wear it when you want to make a bold statement or exude authority. Spiritually, black is complex; some believe it absorbs negative energy or signals protection, while in other traditions, it's seen as attracting bad news or representing mystery and the unknown.

So, next time you pick an outfit, remember that your colors are telling your story on the inside and the outside.

The first step to glamour is feeling confident in your style. Accessories are the real secret to standing out. They make a big difference and help your style stay unique. People who use accessories well always look special. I can wear the same outfit and make it look completely different by changing the accessories. That's why I always say: shop for accessories, especially jewelry—pearls never go out of style. Keep your wardrobe stocked with belts, shoes, bracelets, watches, earrings, necklaces, and bags. These give you endless ways to make every outfit memorable.

Take your time to find the right accessories to match each look. Ask yourself what story you want to tell with each piece: Does this bracelet remind you of a cherished vacation? Does that scarf represent a personal triumph or milestone? These micro-stories add depth to your style and make your choices more intentional.

Accessories are my top secret to glamour. By focusing on these details, you create a style that's memorable and truly yours.

No glamorous look is complete without the perfect accessory. For centuries, people have adorned themselves with natural stones and birthstones—not just for their beauty, but for the unique meanings and personal stories they carry.[69] Whether you choose pearls for their timeless elegance, diamonds for their brilliance, or a birthstone that reflects your journey, each piece adds a layer of sophistication and intention to your style.

Select the stones and accessories that align with your personal style and the narrative you wish to convey. Glamour is not only about appearance. It's about expressing your unique spirit with confidence and intention. Wearing your specific birthstone adds a layer of personal meaning and connection to your look. Understanding the true importance of birthstones, their history, symbolism, and energy allows you to wear them not as decoration, but as a reflection of who you are and what you value. When you understand the meaning behind your birthstone, you know how, why, and when to wear it with glamour, transforming an accessory into a statement of identity and purpose. *A birthstone is more than an accessory—it's a symbol of your journey, a touchstone for your spirit, and a reminder to wear your story with pride.*

According to the International Gem Society and other traditional gemstone guides,[70] here are the birthstones associated with each zodiac sign:

Diamond: Aries (March 21 - April 19)

Emerald: Taurus (April 20 - May 20)

Pearl: Gemini (May 21 - June 20)

Ruby: Cancer (June 21 - July 22)

Peridot: Leo (July 23 - August 22)

Sapphire: Virgo (August 23 - September 22)

Opal: Libra (September 23 - October 22)

Topaz: Scorpio (October 23 - November 21)

Turquoise: Sagittarius (November 22 - December 21)

Garnet: Capricorn (December 22 - January 19)

Amethyst: Aquarius (January 20 - February 18)

Aquamarine: Pisces (February 19 - March 20)

Birthstone Meanings

According to International Gem Society.

Pearl: Purity, innocence, and sincerity.

Aquamarine: Calming, soothing, and cleansing; inspires truth, trust, and letting go.

Diamond: Strength, love, and purity.

Emerald: Rebirth, love, and vitality.

Ruby: Passion, protection, and prosperity.

Peridot: Strength, protection, and healing.

Sapphire: Wisdom, virtue, and good fortune.

Citrine: Prosperity, joy, and energy.

Tanzanite: Transformation and spiritual awakening.

Turquoise: Protection, healing, and communication.

Garnet: Commitment, regeneration, and energy.

Amethyst: Clarity of mind, calm, and protection.

Opal: Inspiration, creativity, and self-expression.

Topaz: Strength, intelligence, and love.

H FOR HUMILITY

Humility is a quiet strength about recognizing the value and importance of every individual and treating others with respect, regardless of their status or background. It's not only about respect—it's about how we interact with others in everyday life, through small gestures and mindful actions. For example, something as simple as cooking your own food, choosing to bike or walk instead of driving when possible, or offering help when you have time, all reflect humility. Judging others or treating people differently based on their appearance or possessions goes against the spirit of being humble. Genuine humility is a memorable habit, rooted in the way we approach each moment and every person we meet.

A similar lesson is highlighted in Eddie Murphy's *Coming to America*. In this comedy, a wealthy prince adopts a modest identity to avoid being judged by his appearance. This causes confusion, resulting in missed opportunities. As an old French proverb says, "Empty barrels make the most noise." It reminds us that it's hard to judge wealth or character by how someone acts or looks. So, let's stay humble and avoid making assumptions about others.

On a personal note, my mother quickly taught us not to waste food growing up. Although my father was often busy, my mother insisted we finish what was on our plates; if not, she would patiently sit with us until we did. She linked food waste to a lack of humility, explaining that many people are hungry. Humble people take only what they need and save the rest for others. I still carry her lesson: *wasting is disrespectful not only to others but also to the universe.* I value what I have and remain mindful of others.

Another lesson in humility comes from traveling through impoverished neighborhoods. A child who witnesses hardship firsthand learns to appreciate what they have and respect every individual, regardless of their circumstances.

To conclude, staying humble means treating everyone with respect, no matter how they look or what they have. By treating others well, regardless of who they are, we open a connection that goes beyond explanation. Once, while I was working at the clothing store, a coworker lost her job for targeting someone she believed was poor based only on their appearance. The customer later complained, and since this was not the first time, she was fired automatically. Humility is not about what you think of someone; it's about recognizing the importance of everyone. With this outlook, we build stronger foundations for personal and professional growth.

I FOR INTERNATIONAL

International words are recognized and used across many languages.[71] They often bring to mind faraway places and varied experiences. Words like "hotel," "taxi," "internet," "restaurant," "café," "radio," "computer," "chocolate," "pizza," "bank," "dollar," and "telephone" come from English, French, Latin, or Greek and are known in business, technology, travel, and food. These shared words help us connect and communicate more easily in a globalized world. If we speak the exact words, might we also share mutual regard? This common vocabulary not only aids in practical communication but also invites us to respect and appreciate the diversity of those we interact with.

Sharing language helps people connect, but nothing can replace an authentic experience. Every country I visit allows me to immerse myself in its people and traditions. Once, while exploring a bustling bazaar in Dakar, I found myself engaged in animated bargaining over vibrant handmade clothes. The merchant, an older adult with a warm smile, shared stories about the craftsmanship and tradition behind each piece. Our exchange wasn't about the price; it was a cultural dance of sorts, revealing nuances of trust, respect, and understanding that no travel guide could capture. In that moment, I discovered that real understanding comes from firsthand exploration. By traveling, you broaden your view and gain richer knowledge beyond what news reports share.

Experienced travelers notice several advantages of travel, including personal growth, exposure to career prospects, cultural experiences, and language learning. Studies show that travel can improve mental health, create lasting memories, and boost creativity.[72] Visiting new places also builds appreciation for diversity, strengthens problem-solving skills, and expands knowledge.[73] On a personal note, one of the most impactful benefits I have experienced is personal growth. While visiting the Leaning Tower of Pisa in Italy, I learned to embrace new perspectives and adapt to unfamiliar situations. This journey not only broadened my view but also enhanced my problem-solving abilities. Through my travels, I can say that it is an entirely different way of learning that everyone should explore.

To make your travel better and less stressful, remember that preparedness can free you to stay present and humble on the road. Consider these general guidelines. While the list is long, it's worth it as it can enhance your journey!

Pack a comprehensive first-aid kit in your suitcase. Divide it into the following categories:

Pain Relief: Include items such as aspirin, Advil, or Tylenol, as well as a basic first-aid ointment.

Digestive Health: Pack Pepto-Bismol (liquid or chewable), MiraLAX or suppositories for constipation, and antacids.

Protective and General Care: Bring hydrocortisone cream for rashes, insect repellent, sunscreen, a thermometer, antiseptic wipes, and safety pins.

Allergies and Minor Ailments: Add antihistamines for allergies, cough drops, and tweezers.

Medical Supplies: Include medical tape, sterile gauze, gloves, a first aid guide, and your prescription medications.

Don't forget to pack more medication than you expect to need. Although the list may be long, this organization ensures peace of mind and safety.

Make all your reservations in advance, including hotels, rental cars, and places to visit, if possible.

Always carry emergency contact information with you (including local emergency numbers and the details of your home country's embassy or consulate).

Always drink bottled or mineral water to avoid stomach issues, especially in countries where tap water isn't safe to drink.

Travel with some cash in local currency, even if you have a bank card or digital payment options—some places may not accept them.

Make photocopies or digital scans of important documents (such as your passport, visa, travel insurance, and credit cards) and keep them separate from the originals.

Keep your valuables secure—use a money belt or hidden pouch and be mindful of pickpockets in crowded areas.

Learn a few basic phrases in the local language—it's helpful and appreciated.

Purchase travel insurance to protect against health issues, accidents, and unexpected changes to your travel plans.

With logistics handled, let's dream. Here are some destinations to inspire your next adventure, each with a bonus piece of information to make your trip even better:

Cultural Places to Visit:

Rome & Pisa (Italy): Museums and iconic architecture. Tip: Purchase tickets for major attractions in advance to avoid long lines.

Côte d'Ivoire: Le Pont des Lianes, meaning The Liana Bridge (Danané and Man), a unique suspension bridge made by spirits at night. There are about 12 of them in the west of Côte d'Ivoire, in the Tonpki region, visited after the Cascades of Man. Tip: Rent a jeep for your trip, as some rural roads can be unpaved and difficult to drive. Wear comfortable shoes and bring water for your hike. Be respectful and greet locals with a friendly "Bonjour."

Senegal (House of Slaves): Powerful history and culture. Tip: Take a guided tour to appreciate the site's significance. Remember to greet locals in Wolof with "Naga def?" to show respect and openness.

France (Paris: Eiffel Tower, Louvre Museum): Landmarks and world-class art. Tip: Visit the Eiffel Tower at sunset for breathtaking views. Engage with Parisians by politely saying "Bonjour" when entering shops or restaurants.

France (Lourdes): Spiritual pilgrimage site with healing waters. Tip: Bring your own empty bottle if you don't want to buy one there to fill with the blessed water. Avoid renting a car. Lourdes is a small city, and some one-way streets change direction every other day. Walking or biking is the best way to explore.

Petra (Jordan): Ancient city carved in stone. Tip: Arrive early to avoid crowds and experience the site in cooler temperatures. Show respect by greeting locals with "As-salamu alaykum."

China (Mount Wuyi, Mogao Caves, Danyang–Kunshan Grand Bridge): Natural and historic marvels. Tip: Respect local customs and be prepared for varied climates. A simple "Nǐ hǎo" can enhance your connections with locals.

Japan (Illuminated Tunnels of Light): Magical Seasonal Displays and Culture. Tip: Check festival dates in advance for the best experience. A gentle bow and a "Konnichiwa" are appreciated gestures.

Cape Town & Table Mountain (South Africa): City life, history, and panoramic views. Tip: Take the cable car up Table Mountain for stunning photos. Learn a few phrases in Afrikaans or Xhosa to show appreciation for cultural diversity.

New York City (USA): World-class museums, Broadway shows, and a memorable dinner at The View Restaurant & Lounge, a revolving rooftop with stunning city views. Tip: Book Broadway tickets and restaurant reservations in advance for the best options.

Beaches & Nature Lovers:

Assinie, La Belle des Sirènes, Monogaga, Île Boulay, Sassandra (Ivory Coast): Beautiful beaches and local flavor. Respect local customs and try fresh seafood from beachside vendors.

Martinique and Guadeloupe (Caribbean): Turquoise waters and island charm. Rent a car to explore hidden beaches and local markets. Greek Islands: Sun-washed villages and crystal coves. Island-hop by ferry for the complete experience.

Bora Bora (French Polynesia): Overwater bungalows and paradise beaches. Splurge on a lagoon tour for unforgettable snorkeling.

Swiss Alps (Switzerland): Majestic mountains and adventure. Dress in layers and always check the weather before hiking.

Grand Canyon (Arizona, USA): An awe-inspiring natural wonder. Visit the South Rim for the most iconic views.

Banff National Park (Canada): Turquoise lakes and mountain scenery. Visit Lake Louise early in the morning to avoid the crowds.

Cascades of Man (Ivory Coast): Spectacular waterfalls. Bring a camera and be prepared for a short hike.

Amazon Rainforest (South America): Biodiversity and adventure. Travel with a reputable guide for added safety and a more enriching experience.

El Nido, Palawan (Philippines): Limestone cliffs and pristine beaches. Book island-hopping tours with local operators for the best value.

Atlantic City (USA): Boardwalk, entertainment, and ocean views. Try the boardwalk's famous saltwater taffy.

Florida Keys (USA): Scenic drives and turquoise waters. Drive the Overseas Highway for spectacular ocean views.

Costa Rica: Rainforests, volcanoes, and eco-adventures. Pack insect repellent, and if you have time, explore both coasts.

Maui (Hawaii, USA): Lush valleys, beaches, and volcanic landscapes. Don't miss the sunrise at Haleakalā National Park.

Tanzania (Africa): Safari in the Serengeti or climb Mount Kilimanjaro. Plan safaris during the Great Migration for an unforgettable wildlife experience.

Romantic Places:

Santorini (Greece): Sunsets and whitewashed villages. Tip: Book a sunset cruise for a magical evening.

Paris (France): The "City of Love" with iconic sights. Tip: Share a picnic by the Seine for a classic romantic moment.

Venice (Italy): Gondola rides and magical canals. Tip: Visit early in the morning or late in the evening to avoid crowds.

Bora Bora (French Polynesia): Perfect for honeymoons. Tip: Opt for an overwater bungalow for the ultimate romantic getaway.

Kyoto (Japan): Cherry blossoms and tranquil temples. Tip: Visit in spring for the best cherry blossom viewing.

Swiss Alps (Switzerland): Cozy chalets and mountain views. Tip: Book a mountain-view room for a cozy retreat.

El Nido, Palawan (Philippines): Secluded beaches and sunsets. Tip: Arrange a private beach dinner for two.

Maldives: Overwater villas and crystal-clear waters. Tip: Plan a couple's spa day for extra relaxation.

Central Park, New York City (USA): Carriage rides, rowboats, and romantic city moments. Tip: Visit Bow Bridge for a picture-perfect scene.

Many people recognize countries by their food even before their flags. Use iconic dishes as anchors: Ivory Coast's Attiéké with fried fish or Alloco (fried plantains) with fish, and palm nut stew with foutou and Kedjenou. What might tasting Attiéké teach you about Ivorian daily life? France's cassoulet with a baguette and crêpes; Spain's empanadillas; Mexico's tacos; Jamaica's jerk chicken with rice and beans; the United States' macaroni and cheese with collard greens and fried chicken; Senegal's Tchep (Thieboudienne). Consider how the communal nature of sharing a bowl of Tchep reflects Senegal's social fabric. Italy's pizza and spaghetti; Belgium's steak frites; India's butter chicken and chana masala; Haiti's patties. As you savor these foods, ponder the stories and histories they carry. Advice: *Try a local dish wherever you go; food makes places memorable!*

Good to know: Around the world, some of the most expensive foods include Almas caviar, Kobe and Wagyu beef, saffron, matsutake mushrooms, bluefin tuna, bird's nest soup, Kopi Luwak coffee, Manuka and "Elvish" honey, moose milk cheese, and white truffles.[74]

Among the world's priciest wines, you'll find Leroy Musigny Grand Cru (Côte de Nuits) and Leroy Domaine d'Auvenay's Chevalier Montrachet and Criots Bâtard Montrachet (Côte de Beaune), all from France.[75] If those are out of reach, a well-made Bordeaux is a classic choice. Wine's alcohol content varies by style and fermentation.

Let these destinations, foods, and experiences inspire you to see more, taste more, and understand the incredible world around us. Humility is the souvenir that outlasts any postcard, leaving a lasting imprint long after the journey ends.

J FOR JOURNAL

Journal helps capture important events and thoughts as they happen. According to Kate Beddow, journaling is an excellent way to preserve memories.[76] My father recorded every event by date and time in his journal, impressing me with his detailed memory. He always consulted his journal before speeches or when answering questions. Once, while we were about to discuss something important, he called my mother to bring his journal. The familiar, comforting scent of ink filled the room as my mother handed it to him. During our discussion, the gentle rustling of pages accompanied his search for dates and facts. Watching him showed me the value of keeping a journal. Even though my father could remember details well, he taught me that journaling makes memories last by turning details into wisdom.

I didn't always have a pen or a journal on hand to take notes, so I started using pictures and screenshots to record events and details. Later,

I used my phone's Notes app. Whether you use digital or handwritten notes, the important thing is to have a way to record what matters. Over time, these notes can become stories to share.

Ideas often go away when we're distracted, so relying only on memory can lead to missed opportunities. Instead, take notes, as what you write today can become tomorrow's wisdom. I recall a time when a brilliant idea flashed in my mind during my commute, only for it to vanish by the time I reached my desk. Without having jotted it down, that idea remained lost, reminding me of the importance of capturing every thought promptly. Kidlin's Law states that "If you write a problem down clearly and specifically, you've solved half of it." [77] Taking time to organize your ideas in this way can help you take charge of your knowledge and improve your life." [78] Journaling gives clarity when facing challenges and can reveal solutions as you write.[79]

According to Psychology Today, journaling can boost well-being, creativity, memory, and motivation while reducing stress. Your journal always listens, remembers, and can guide you.

Writing about your day and important facts helps you notice changes and find solutions. Journaling lets you learn from mistakes, remember ideas, and improve your writing skills. Over time, your notes might become a memoir or an inspiring story.[80] *Even the faintest ink outlasts the strongest memory.81*

Journaling isn't only about recording events. It helps you capture ideas, learn from experience, and build a resource to revisit. Use photos, digital notes, or paper—choose what works for you. Your journal can become a key tool for growth, creativity, and success.

K FOR KNOWLEDGE

Knowledge was at the heart of Cleopatra's power. Have you ever heard the story of Cleopatra, the legendary queen of Egypt? Cleopatra was renowned not only for her beauty but also for her intelligence, strategic thinking, and ability to influence powerful leaders, such as Julius Caesar and Mark Antony.[82] Through her mastery of languages, diplomacy, and political acumen, Cleopatra secured her position and shaped the destiny of her kingdom.[83] Her influence stemmed not only from her wealth but also from her relentless pursuit of knowledge and her ability to apply it effectively. [84] Her ability to master her environment and adapt with agility serves as a timeless leadership lesson: understanding and commanding the context in which one operates can significantly multiply one's influence and leverage.

When we talk about knowledge in this chapter, we mean much more than what you learn in school or from textbooks. Knowledge is anything that helps you in life—useful information, hands-on experience, problem-solving skills, and lessons picked up from everyday situations and from specialized fields. It's not limited to what teachers present in a classroom. Instead, it's also about what you choose to look for and learn on your own, whether that's a new skill, a life lesson, or an insight from talking with someone. For example, architects and designers rely on their ability to picture spaces in their minds, while counselors and managers depend on their people skills and empathy. Some of the most important lessons come from reflecting on your own feelings, motivations, and choices. In short, knowledge is a mix of learning from life, practicing new things, and being curious enough to seek what matters to you—even if it's never been taught in a classroom.

Learning is easier than ever, but competition is fierce. Choose carefully what you want to learn. The content you consume shapes your opportunities. Like Cleopatra, be intentional about the knowledge you pursue for growth and influence.

There's an important distinction between being "book smart" and "street smart." In my chapter on education, I highlighted that we need both to truly succeed. Book smarts usually refer to academic knowledge—what you learn in school, from books, or through formal study. Street smarts are gained through real-world experience: navigating challenges, reading people, solving problems on the fly, and adapting quickly.[85] You won't get the same result if you give the same assignment to someone who is only street smart versus someone who is only book smart. But *the best results often come from those who have both—the practical knowledge of street smarts combined with the academic foundation of book smarts.* I witnessed this firsthand in my role as a supervisor, where I conducted candidate interviews. One thing that worked for me during interviews was taking the time to build a genuine connection with people—helping them relax and open up about who they are. When I did this, I noticed something important: the people who had both book smarts and street smarts always seemed to shine. They memorized not only answers—they thought things through, handled surprises with ease, and spoke with real confidence. In the end, those who succeed are not smart in one way—they're completely smart, bringing together the best of both worlds.

The most valuable knowledge for anyone is knowing a little more about what matters. That can make a big difference when you need to decide and manage your life without a coach. Some of us may need a life coach to take the next step—but with knowledge and an understanding of ourselves and our surroundings, we have access to everything we need to improve and move forward as far as we want. With knowledge, we can make informed decisions and effect change.

Wilson's Law states, "If you put information first at all times, then the money keeps coming."[86] Focus on knowledge and openness to learning—this is the root of future progress. Growing each day, and success will follow.

Actual knowledge starts at home. Share your story, values, and discipline openly with your children by explaining the why behind every decision. Also, when your kids watch you, they pick up your habits and are inspired by your actions. Let them see your best version—share your experiences and guide them with honesty and care. One of the best ways to teach is by inviting them into your thought process. For example, you might ask, 'Why do you think I budget our grocery money this way?' Questions like these not only get them involved but also help them understand the reasons behind everyday choices.

What I learned at home had the most profound impact on me. My parents taught with openness and stories. I choose to do the same—sharing lessons without hesitation, believing it always makes a difference. Knowledge lives in what we share and model daily.

L FOR LANGUAGE

language usage—even a few phrases—and some cultural knowledge shows real effort and genuine desire to connect. Language is a powerful bridge; this effort builds trust, closes business deals, and starts friendships. It shows care and a willingness to meet others where they are. However, not knowing even a word of their language can quickly create distance instead of connection.

Accents are an essential aspect of language and identity. Every region has a distinct sound: Florida isn't California; New York isn't Georgia. The U.S. is not alone—English varies globally: the UK, Canada, Liberia, and South Africa have unique accents and rhythms, as French sounds different in Canada than in France or Belgium. Culture shapes how we speak, so understanding culture matters—in English or any language.

Have you noticed the first question after meeting someone is often, "Where are you from?" or "What's your accent?" It's better to wait until after a few conversations. To foster comfort, listen first, or share which languages you speak and ask which they prefer. This is more welcoming.

Language is more than words; it includes verbal, nonverbal, visual, and written forms. Nonverbal communication is interesting, so we must remain mindful of it to maintain clear, respectful interactions.

There are 10 methods of nonverbal communication: facial expressions, gestures, paralinguistics (voice), proxemics (personal space), eye contact, touch, appearance, posture, chronemics (time), and physiological responses. Experts emphasize that most communication is nonverbal: tone, body language, and signals convey meaning beyond words.[87]

Improving nonverbal cues—such as smiling, an open posture, and patience—helps foster meaningful interactions, even across language barriers.

To improve nonverbal communication: use good posture, stay aware, make simple eye contact, and manage your responses.

Quick guide: Arms crossed means defensiveness; Looking down or face turned away means disbelief or disengagement; Stroking chin means thinking or deciding;

One arm across body means shyness/self-comfort; Hands on hips means ready/controlling (can read as aggressive); Eyebrows raised means interest/attention/surprise (sometimes flirting). [88]

Understanding body language lets you avoid unnecessary conflict and foster harmony in relationships. Your body speaks—make sure it says what you mean. Remember: most of what we "say" is beyond words.

According to Ethnologue.com, there are 196 countries and 7,159 languages spoken worldwide. When we look at language distribution by region, the numbers are striking. Africa has 2,294 languages; Europe has 287; and the Americas have 1,061.[89] These facts highlight the importance of understanding body language and nonverbal cues, as well as mastering the ability to connect with a wide variety of people. The words you use reach only a small group. Once we travel and discover the wider world, we often rely more on nonverbal communication: facial expressions, tone, posture, and presence. To communicate respect and build trust. When we express ourselves both verbally and nonverbally, we can connect with anyone.

M FOR MANNERS

Manners start with words like "thank you," "please," "excuse me," "I'm sorry," and "my apologies"—used worldwide to show respect. Using them daily shows good manners and reflects well on your character. Honoring diverse cultures, traditions, and beliefs is a sign of respect. Living by ethics and standards gains respect and shows integrity in a world hungry for authenticity.

Demonstrate good manners through simple, thoughtful communication every day. When someone speaks—even in tough conversations—listen closely before responding. Many reply before fully listening. Be patient; sometimes repeat or paraphrase to show you understand. Communication fails when someone stops listening. Even if you're a boss, listen to employees—those on the floor often have valuable insights.

An example of good manners: When using a public bathroom at work or elsewhere, always clean up after yourself. This should be second nature, but unfortunately, it's often overlooked. Of course, you're not expected to clean up someone else's mess, but if you find the bathroom dirty, please let the next person know it was in that condition. If you say nothing, they may believe you left it dirty. It's also helpful to alert the cleaning team right away—whether you're in a store or at work, there's usually a housekeeping team you can call to address the situation. Walking away saying nothing often means you're contributing to the problem.

To recap, good manners foster comfort and respect. Important points: Learn and use people's names; never shout them across a room.

Put your phone away during meals.

Never go where you have not been invited.

Be on time.

Keep the noise down in quiet places—especially libraries.

Clean up after yourself (home, office, public spaces).

If you're sick, keep your distance and cover your mouth (use your elbow/shoulder).

Ask guests about food allergies before serving meals.

Knock before entering the rooms or homes of friends or family members. Give notice before visiting a friend.

Hold the door for the person behind you— and they should do the same for the next person.

A man should always open the door for his lady.

Allow the person who calls you to discuss the reason for their call before you do.

Ladies should sit with a straight, graceful posture and cross their legs at the ankles.[90]

Men should sit with both feet flat on the floor.

Social media is not a platform for degrading others; use it to inform, uplift, or stay in touch.

Never bring an extra guest when invited without prior permission— always RSVP as indicated.

Never waste food. If you have enough, share it; if you can't share, dispose of it properly.

A classy person never bullies. Bullying signals insecurity and unhappiness.

Learn the names of the people who serve you.

 Use proper etiquette (good manners), including excusing yourself before leaving the table. Never pick your nose, ears, or attempt to remove anything from your mouth at the table. If you need to tend to any personal matters, excuse yourself to use the bathroom.

Don't burp at the table. If that happens, cover your mouth and apologize.

Always wait for everyone to be served and seated at the table before you eat.

When facing real scenarios what to do?

Most likely: Pause → Speak once (calmly) → Redirect/Exit → Follow up privately (if needed).

Forget someone's name.
"I'm sorry—please remind me of your name." If needed, reintroduce them to someone so their name is repeated.

Wrong restaurant order
Quietly flag the server: "I think there was a mix-up." Be clear, patient, and discreet.

Colleague takes credit
In the moment: "Glad it's resonating—let me add context since I developed it." Address privately afterward; document.

Overdressed
Own it. No apologies. If commented on: "I like to dress up." Move on.

Underdressed
Stay confident. No self-mockery. Be present and engaged; note the dress code for next time.

A friend asks for money.
Only give what you can afford to lose. Decide:
gift or loan. If no: "I can't right now, but I'm
rooting for you."

Gift you don't like!
Thank them sincerely: "That's thoughtful."
Focus on the relationship, not the item.

The menu is unfamiliar.
Ask well: "What do you recommend if I like
lighter flavors?" Curiosity beats pretending.

Home is not clean
Say nothing. Act normal. No commentary, no
gossip later.

Family embarrasses you in public.
Don't match energy. Redirect or step aside.
Address privately later.

Asked how much you paid
Deflect gracefully: "It was a great find." You
don't owe financial details.

Networking event—know no one.
Arrive early. Stand where people circulate.
Introduce yourself. Aim for 1–2 real
conversations, then follow up.

Date rude to the waiter
Be warm to the waiter. Later, privately: "How
we treat service staff matters to me."

Exit a conversation
Close cleanly: "Lovely talking—I'm going to

say hello to a few people. Let's stay in touch."
Then leave.

Uninvited guest at your home
Warm but firm: "What a surprise—I'm not set
up for company." Brief visit only. If repeated,
set a boundary.

Catch someone in a lie (public)
Don't expose them publicly. Note it. Address
privately if it affects you or causes harm.

Food or anything on someone's face/clothes
Immediately: give them eye contact and show
them by a simple gesture on your own face,
pointing to the part. Discreet kindness. Vice
versa, when someone looks at you and keeps
touching a specific part of their body, they are
telling you that something needs to be fixed
on that part of the body.

The meeting runs long; you must leave.
State clearly: "I have a hard stop at [time]. Let's
cover the most critical points before I go."
(Ideally said at the start.)

Witness poor treatment; want to intervene.
Intervene immediately, and remove the target
with dignity: "Can I steal you for a moment?"
Don't ignore injustice and report in
accordingly.

You make a public mistake: Recover fast: brief
humor, fix what you can, apologize only if
needed, move on.

Good manners also mean adapting to the house rules and the culture you're entering. When visiting someone's home, ask questions, including whether you should remove your shoes and wash your hands before entering. Listening first, asking politely, and respecting customs signal care and class.

Have you ever heard that "it is not what you say, but how you say it"– it's all about manners? I believe one rose coming from the right person is worth a thousand roses coming from the wrong person, and one genuine smile coming from the right person is worth a thousand fake smiles. Learning and practicing good manners makes a big difference and gives you value that can never be bought.

Another great option is to build your own manners library or rules. You can start by reading a book about etiquette. There are many excellent books on etiquette. Read at least one and keep practicing.

N FOR NAVIGATING

Navigating is not just about transformation; it's about making the most of what you have. Making French "crêpes"? You need flour, milk, salt, butter, and eggs. If I'm out of eggs or butter, I can still make crêpes. If I'm out of milk or salt, I can manage. But no flour means no crêpes. Flour is fundamental. I realized I am the 'flour' in my recipe. Prioritizing my health and well-being allows me to face any challenge and keep moving forward. Same as flour in Crêpes, our well-being is essential to our life's recipe. Examine what's on your menu and work with what you have, because sometimes the ingredients aren't all there.

Life can be tough, but what matters most is how you see things, how you understand them, and how you choose to respond. Recognizing your own capacity to navigate challenges is crucial, as it sets the tone for overcoming adversity with resilience and grace.

When I moved to New York without my parents, I cried every night because I missed them, and everything felt new. Living with my parents, I never had to wash dishes, do laundry, or clean, since I always had help. Suddenly, I had to do it all myself. Even though my school was paid for, I wanted to return to Abidjan. I felt shame for not coping better, fear for what lay ahead, and loneliness amidst the city's hustle. Making new friends and keeping in touch with my family helped me adjust. I often felt lost, as if I was watching my life from the outside, hoping things would get easier. Even years later, I missed my parents and felt like every day was the same, because my happiest moments had always been with them.

I learned to follow my passions by welcoming change. Still, I often felt stuck between wanting to give up and wanting to keep going. To overcome these feelings, I developed a simple routine that gave me strength and focus. Each morning, I would wake up early and take a quiet moment to read the original book of Psalms my father gave me and reflect on a step toward my larger ambitions. Every psalm was like making a new friend. This practice helped me see progress, no matter how small; each step kept me moving forward, even when I felt overwhelmed. Whenever I faced a big decision, I reminded myself to read my psalms. Interestingly, things got better when I found new friends /family in

New York. It was like adding a new ingredient to a recipe and having it finally come together. With new friends and skills, I learned to adapt and keep moving forward.

One memory with my parents stands out. I had to perform a classical dance for my school, and the teacher wanted each of us to hold a large lollipop. It wasn't a regular one—it had to be specially ordered because of its size. My parents were busy and hadn't ordered it in time. The day before the show, we searched everywhere: bakeries, supermarkets, and more. We finally found one, but it was broken in half. My parents bought it anyway, and I went to the show with my broken lollipop. I was disappointed and stayed quiet on the way to school. But during the performance, I danced with so much joy that the broken lollipop became part of the show and a memory I'll never forget. My parents were so proud of me. *Accurate navigation isn't about having a perfect plan; it's about trusting yourself to keep going, even when things are uncertain.*

My father said, "This is for fun, Berthille. You must be a doctor, not a dancer." He wanted me to know the difference between passion and profession. As a child, I didn't see the bigger picture. I stopped classical dance for another reason, but I never went back to it, and I still feel like something is missing. This taught me that no matter how busy you are, it's essential to make time for your passions. Doing what you love is essential for your well-being and growth. This memory also reminds me that anyone can move from disappointment to happiness, and having many talents is a gift. It can feel like a lot to handle, but it's also powerful. It's like caring for different children; you need to make time for each one, the same as you should for your talents.

Later, my parents visited me in NYC and stayed for a few months. When they returned to Abidjan a year later, my father passed away. As I was navigating through that pain, my mother passed away three months after he did. Suddenly, my most precious parents were gone. I couldn't have navigated that time without my husband, who was fully there for me. Unfortunately, he also passed away two years later. I thought I couldn't continue with any more pain or even try to navigate life. I believed that what remained was not enough to keep going. I was certain I could not go on. At that point, I took a two-month break from work to stay with my sibling in Abidjan. When I returned to NYC, I went back to work and continued to navigate life. Sometimes things go well, and sometimes they don't. But whatever happens, I learned to keep moving forward, no matter how much it hurts. Eventually, I noticed that the love I had for each of them was so strong that it alone gave me the courage I needed to navigate each day. When you learn to navigate, you discover that *every change in life is an invitation to navigate with courage. Embrace what you have and find strengths you never knew you had.*

Another experience for me was working two jobs while going to school. At one point, I had to choose my job over my studies, but I eventually finished my education. Sometimes, navigating means deciding what you need most to move forward. Navigating life means adapting, setting priorities, and believing you can keep going, no matter what changes come your way. When you learn to navigate, you become stronger and more resourceful. Consider choosing a routine that reinforces these principles by adding a habit to your life.

Thinking about "nobility," I realized that real nobility is about character and integrity, especially when times are tough. Life's challenges show that dignity and kindness are more important than titles or status.

Have you ever seen or read the play "Le Bourgeois Gentilhomme" by the French writer Molière? It cleverly and humorously shows the class differences between nobles and the middle class. The play is both interesting and funny. It also shows how values and social classes can get mixed up. In the end, it's our values that define us, not our titles or what society thinks.

Changing your name is another way of navigating life. At one point, I considered changing my name because it was long and made introductions difficult. But deep down, I love my name. I realized that changing it could hurt my parents and our culture, so I kept it and work on presenting myself better. Many people change their names for various reasons, such as historical reasons, similarity, or to escape the legacy of slavery.[91] Whatever your reason, think about the history—sometimes names repeat stories and shape our reality. When choosing a name for your child, check its meaning to make sure it won't have a negative effect. Seeing or hearing the same thing every day can influence you, so be aware of how names can affect anyone's life.[92] I almost called this chapter "Name," but chose "Navigate" to talk about bigger changes and different ways of navigating.

Sometimes, I've found it hard to move from one responsibility to another, but the more I think about it, the more I see we are all navigators. On some days, I might start my morning as a parent, carefully aligning my tone to encourage my children as they get ready for school. Then, at work, I switch gears to present a more assertive posture during a business meeting, using precise language to lead a project discussion. Later in the evening, I might meet with friends, adopting a relaxed and light-hearted attitude. Each transition requires a shift in language and demeanor to suit the context. As friends, children, parents, or professionals, we play different roles and use different ways of speaking depending on where we are and who we're with. We naturally adjust our attitudes to fit each situation. To better control your life, you need to navigate well, whether you're a counselor, a customer service representative, a nurse, or a business owner. Navigating well helps you succeed in every role. It's a valuable skill for any goal. *To navigate isn't only to move; it's adapting, growing, and becoming your best self, wherever life takes you.*

O FOR ORIGINAL

Original means being true to yourself. It's not only about being yourself but also making choices that reflect authenticity. Likewise, select original products rather than fake alternatives. So, please stop carrying and wearing counterfeit designer items—it's not classy. Don't copy other people's work; give yourself credit for your own style. Wearing a fake LV bag or Hermès-branded shoes signals insecurity and intimidation.93 Buy what you can afford and wear it with pride. Society doesn't need to see a logo to respect you. In fact, choosing authenticity is a major step toward being truly classy. Learn how to spot fakes versus the real thing—reliable guides and comparisons are widely available on reputable sites and video platforms. Authenticity is elegance.

Looks might catch our attention, but what keeps us connected is being real and feeling comfortable. Imagine meeting someone who seems attractive at first, but then you find out their hair, teeth, face, body, or even skin tone has been changed. At what point do we stop changing ourselves? What feels right to you? Before considering changes, take a moment to reflect on two things you already like about your natural appearance. How do you show confidence in your natural self?

Lightening or changing your skin color isn't necessary—it can be harmful. Instead, take care of your natural skin by keeping it hydrated, using excellent products, wearing sunscreen, and eating well. Every skin color is beautiful; someone else was born with the look you're trying to copy.

With makeup, try to keep it light so there are no surprises when you take it off. A little can highlight your features, but real confidence attracts others. Whether you wear no makeup or use it to express yourself, remember that clothes and accessories are part of how you look—don't let makeup hide who you are. Always make sure your products are safe and gentle for your skin.

Artists and creators are often the ones most hurt by counterfeiting and plagiarism. Always give credit to the original creator when you use or mention someone's work; it shows respect for their craft and protects their rights. Don't support the sale or purchase of fake items—when we buy fakes, we add to the problem. If no one buys counterfeits, plagiarists lose their market. Just as we cite sources in school, we should credit artists, scientists, and researchers in daily life.

How to Recognize Real Gold:

Genuine gold doesn't tarnish or fade, while the fakes may discolor. Look for stamps like "10K," "14K," "18K," "22K," or "24K"—these are good signs you've got the real thing. If you hold it near a magnet and it sticks, it's likely not real gold since genuine gold isn't magnetic. Genuine gold also feels heavier and denser than most imitations. When in doubt, jewelers can use an acid test—genuine gold won't react with the acid.94

How to Recognize Real Silver:

Genuine silver is usually marked with "925," "Sterling," or ".925." If you notice poor or missing stamps, it may be a counterfeit. Like gold, genuine silver isn't magnetic. It will tarnish and turn dark over time, but that can be polished away; fakes may chip or peel instead. Tap it gently; genuine silver, creates a high-pitched ring. Silver testing kits can also help confirm the diagnosis.95

How to Recognize a Real Diamond:

Try the fog test: breathe on the stone—real diamonds disperse heat quickly and won't fog up, while fakes might stay cloudy for a few seconds. Diamonds can scratch glass, so that's another quick check. Under a magnifying glass, real diamonds have sharp edges and natural imperfections; fake diamonds often appear too perfect. Drop your stone in water—real diamonds will sink because they're dense. Many real diamonds also glow blue under UV light.96

How to Recognize a Real Luxury Watch:

A genuine luxury watch typically feels heavier because it's crafted from high-quality materials. Watch the second hand: genuine watches often have a smooth, sweeping motion, while fakes usually tick. Look for crisp, clean engravings and unique, traceable serial numbers. Authentic watches typically use sapphire crystal, gold, or high-grade steel, whereas fakes often employ cheaper materials. And if the price seems too good to be true, chances are it is fake.97

How to Recognize a Genuine Designer Bag:

Check the stitching—authentic designer bags have even, precise stitches, while fakes often have loose threads or uneven lines. High-quality leather or fabric is a hallmark of authenticity; fakes might use plastic or low-grade materials. The hardware should feel solid and weighty, with engraved logos, not just painted metal. Logos and labels should be crisp and correctly spelled. Authentic bags typically come with unique serial numbers and authenticity cards, as well as branded dust bags and packaging.98

Fabric Guide (Most to Least Expensive) Satin is renowned for its luxurious sheen and smooth texture. High-quality satin is often made from silk, making it one of the pricier options.99 It's typically used for evening bags, special occasion garments, or premium linings. Satin looks elegant but can be delicate and prone to snags.

Leather: Genuine leather is a classic choice for bags and accessories. It's durable, ages beautifully, and can be expensive, depending on the grade (full-grain is the best). Leather is often regarded as the gold standard for quality and durability. 100

Cotton: A natural fiber that's soft, breathable, and comfortable. It's used in everything from everyday bags to high-quality clothing. While not as expensive as leather or silk-based satin, good cotton can still be a sign of quality—especially if it's organic or tightly woven.

Vinyl (Faux Leather): A synthetic material designed to mimic the appearance of leather. It's much more affordable and easier to clean, but it doesn't last as long and can crack or peel over time. Vinyl is often used in budget-friendly bags and accessories.

Polyester: A widely used synthetic fiber. It's lightweight, durable, and very affordable, but it doesn't have the luxurious feel of natural fibers. Polyester is popular for casual bags, linings, and fast fashion items.101

Quality Recommendation: For the best quality and longevity, genuine leather is often the top choice for bags and accessories, thanks to its exceptional durability and timeless appeal. For clothing, high-quality cotton or silk-based satin offers both comfort and elegance. Polyester and vinyl are budget-friendly but don't offer the same feel or lifespan as natural fabrics.102 For everyday use, opt for leather or sturdy cotton. For special occasions, satin or silk can add a luxurious touch. Always check the stitching and overall construction—quality craftsmanship matters as much as the fabric itself.

P FOR POSTURE

Posture plays a critical role in personal presentation. Sitting and standing with proper alignment show both confidence and respect. For women, maintaining legs together, arms relaxed, and a straight back conveys poise. For men, keeping both feet flat and maintaining an upright position is recommended. Observing interesting examples can facilitate learning. Use posture intentionally to communicate confidence and refinement in any environment.

To improve posture, consider taking a movement class, such as classical dance or acting. These provide clear guidance on purposeful movement. Before public appearances, visualize and plan your posture and gestures. These nonverbal cues show engagement and intent. Practice the signals you want to convey.

Acting classes made me more aware of my posture and body language. Audiences notice if you are genuine. If you depend too much on mirrors, you might come across as fake. Instead, build real self-awareness to appear authentic. Social learning shows that people pick up new behaviors, attitudes, and feelings by watching and copying others [103]

In important meetings, your posture and facial expression are a big part of your professional image. They affect how others see you. Always try to look calm and put-together to have a polished look.

Posture and Gesture Guide: Quick Tips to Remember

Sit: Hips back in the chair, spine tall, shoulders down, chin parallel to the floor.

Stand: Feet grounded, weight centered, ribs stacked over hips, neck long.

Hands: Keep gestures below the shoulders, smooth and purposeful.

Face: Soft eyes, slight natural smile; avoid frowning or darting gaze.

Space: Respect personal space; angle your body slightly instead of squaring off.

Spine: Tall, ribs over hips, neck long; shoulders down and back.

Feet: Grounded; avoid rocking or pacing without purpose.

Gestures: Keep them below the shoulders and slow slightly on key points.

Eye contact: Hold eye contact for 3 to 5 seconds, then look away for a moment before returning.

Microexpressions: Relax the brow and jaw to avoid an unintended "stern" look.

Bonus tip: When you enter a room, pause for a moment, stand tall, and make gentle eye contact with someone before you sit down. This simple step can boost your confidence and help you feel more aware.

Good posture is important for your health. It also shows others you are healthy and confident. People notice if someone limps, pauses often, or has trouble moving. These signs can mean discomfort or health problems. If you have medical issues that affect your mobility, talk to a specialist. Make daily exercise part of your routine to help your health and posture.

People notice every detail when you present. How you look and what's around you matter. Distractions can weaken your message, so pay attention to your entire presentation.

Today, many people give presentations online, but sometimes forget to check their background first. Even experienced speakers show professionalism by preparing carefully, including how they look before they start.

Dressing well and carrying yourself with confidence helps you attract and keep your audience.

Always get ready carefully before any presentation. Practice with professionals if you can. If possible, ask someone to check your appearance for any mistakes or distractions. Paying attention to these details helps you make a good impression with the correct posture.

Q FOR QUALITY

Quality over quantity is a timeless mantra that elevates every area of life. While it may cost more upfront, prioritizing quality ensures a more durable, satisfying, and enjoyable journey. Think of booking a bargain bed-and-breakfast only to find unkempt surroundings that spoil the stay or buying clothing that falls apart after a single wear. Embracing quality transforms ordinary moments into sources of joy. Well-made choices pay you back every day.

When you make an informed choice, you feel confident. You won't doubt yourself while shopping. Take your time. Look up options, read reviews, and ask people who have tried the product. Learn the details before you buy. Every purchase, even food, deserves your attention.

Quality also saves you time. Cheap items often lead to extra returns, repairs, replacements, and customer service issues. If you choose well the first time, you save time and avoid stress.

Quality is more than a price—it's peace of mind and time saved.

Scrutinize labels and dates. Choose high-quality ingredients to nourish body and spirit. By prioritizing quality in every transaction, you invest not only in better goods but in your own well-being. Let your choices enrich your life and resonate with excellence.

Going out to eat? Ask friends you trust and check reliable guides to find places with excellent service and safe, tasty food. Picking the right spot helps you enjoy good food and conversation with no surprises. Choose restaurants that value your time, health, and taste.

Sometimes, quality means picking what fits the moment. Not every quality item lasts forever, and that's fine. For example, fresh flowers look beautiful for about two weeks, then fade. This doesn't mean you shouldn't give flowers—it means you should match your gift to the occasion. If you want something that lasts, try a living plant. It's a gift with roots, not petals. Let your gifts have meaning and lasting value.

Quality isn't about luxury; it's about making thoughtful choices that improve your health, happiness, and success. Use these practical tips as a guide to elevate your everyday decisions:

Perfume and cologne are about more than smell. They also need to last, use safe ingredients, and work nicely on your skin. Don't mix up "eau de cologne," which is lighter, with "eau de parfum," which is stronger and lasts longer. Good fragrances use quality ingredients and shift throughout the day. Cheaper ones may fade fast or smell fake. With a pleasant scent, you can use less and enjoy a more authentic experience.

Cosmetic products require special attention to ingredient safety. Some dangerous chemicals to avoid include parabens, formaldehyde, formaldehyde-releasing preservatives such as DMDM hydantoin, phthalates, lead, mercury, and benzene. These can be linked to allergies, hormone disruption, and even cancer.[104] It's wise to check if a product is cruelty-free and to look for transparent ingredient lists. Trusted brands are transparent about their ingredients and are often certified by reputable organizations, such as the Leaping Bunny or PETA.[105] Be aware of recalls, as cosmetics can be pulled from shelves for contamination or undisclosed ingredients, and using recalled products can put your health at risk. For up-to-date information on recalls and consumer safety, consult official sources such as the FDA or the Consumer Product Safety Commission.

Providers and clothing retailers remind us that with clothing, quality often depends on the brand name. Therefore, you need to research every brand. It's not about showing off a brand name as a signature. It's about understanding what each brand stands for: their standards, values, and commitment to quality. Discover the reputation and philosophy that underpin a brand. This helps you choose clothing that reflects the standard and uniqueness you want. Whether you shop at a factory retailer, boutique, or tailor, remember that special occasions may call for exclusivity. Everyday workwear can benefit from professional design and unique mix-and-match choices. The fashion industry is full of imitation. Select brands renowned for their exceptional cuts and distinctive style.

Wine and champagne represent quality made from varieties of grapes, like the wines from Bordeaux (France). True champagne must come from the Champagne region of France. Look for "Champagne" on the label.[106] Quality wines and champagnes have depth, complexity, and a clean finish, while lower-quality options can taste flat or overly sweet. Some sparkling wines are labeled "champagne" even though they don't meet the standards. Quality here means more enjoyment and fewer headaches.

Services, including hotels, restaurants, amusement parks, and Airbnb, are about more than the taste of the food or a comfortable bed. Look for a clean environment, attentive and knowledgeable staff, and a menu that's focused and seasonal. High-quality restaurants provide clear allergen information, maintain consistency during both peak and off-peak hours, and offer a comfortable noise level that facilitates conversation. They also value your time— service is prompt but never rushed, and reservations or wait times are communicated honestly.[107] For hotels, quality means clean rooms, comfortable beds, good amenities, and responsive customer service. Amusement parks and Airbnb stays should prioritize safety, organization, and guest satisfaction above all else. Before booking or visiting, always check recent reviews, policies, and guest feedback to ensure you're getting the experience you expect. Choosing quality in services means fewer unpleasant surprises and more memorable moments. When evaluating restaurants and services, consider the reputation of people you trust, recent reviews, cleanliness, staff attentiveness, allergen awareness, a focused, seasonal menu, a conversational noise level, and consistency across both peak and off-peak times. Always read policies, survey photos, verify reviews, and compare warranties.

Food and water are central to your health and well-being. Choose supermarkets that prioritize quality fresh produce, clear labeling, clean aisles, and knowledgeable staff. Quality food means fewer chemicals, better nutrition, and real flavor. Poor food choices can directly affect your health; processed snacks and sugary treats may be convenient, but they increase your risk of illness over time. For water, filter systems are often preferable to relying on plastic bottles, as plastics can leach chemicals into the water over time.[108] The quality of what you eat and drink every day is directly connected to your health, energy, and long-term wellness. Simple swaps, such as choosing an apple over a bag of cookies, can make a big difference.

Electronics like TVs, washers, dryers, computers, phones, or video gear, quality matters. For TVs, look for the latest features, such as smart functions, 4K or 8K resolution, HDR, and streaming. Good washers and dryers are energy-saving, quiet, and last longer, while cheap ones may break or use more energy. Computers and phones with high-quality parts work better, last longer, and receive updates, while cheaper ones may slow down or become outdated quickly. Video equipment with high-quality lenses and sensors produces clearer images and lasts longer.[109] Choosing quality over quantity in electronics saves you money and trouble in the long run.

When choosing a car, think about reliability, safety, and how well it fits your needs. Consider your climate, how far you drive, your family size, and your budget. Keeping up with maintenance is important—skipping it can cost more later. Any car can get you where you need to go, but a well-chosen, well-cared-for car does it safely and efficiently. The more you invest in quality and care, the more value and peace of mind you get. Always pick what best fits your situation.

To conclude this chapter, read the label before it meets your body or reaches your throat. If you can read, you can start building the habit of making smart, quality-focused decisions that will reward you for years to come. Make it a habit to read every label that comes into contact with your skin, hair, and lungs, and especially the label on your food. When in doubt, take a clear photo of the ingredient list and research ingredient to understand its benefits and risks. Some products won't disclose everything; that's your cue to research brand standards or choose a more transparent option. Quality is selecting the right kind of lasting benefits. Create your personal "quality standards" and stick to them: a short list of non-negotiables, such as materials, warranty, sourcing, and safety. Please keep it on your phone and check it before making a purchase. Making an excellent choice doesn't require expert knowledge. Always take recalls seriously. If you live in the USA, check CPSC.gov/Recalls for product safety alerts and ConsumerFinance.gov/complaint to report issues or learn more about consumer rights. Over time, this becomes a signature of your lifestyle. People will notice that your things last and your choices feel intentional. Standards make your style recognizable and reliable.

R FOR READY

Ready means being prepared to handle unexpected, last-minute events. Whether it's a spontaneous gathering or an impromptu outing, always be ready for the next step. Imagine your life as a movie—would you want to be surprised, looking disheveled at the supermarket or sloppy on your front porch? Keep a range of clothing options—from comfy pajamas to polished outfits for special occasions—and keep hair and face well-groomed so you don't need a last-minute salon run. Dress appropriately for the occasion and move with quiet confidence.

Change your clothes throughout the day to match your plans: work clothes, casual wear, and pajamas for sleep. Don't stay in pajamas all day or sleep in clothes you wore outside. Make this a daily habit to show respect for yourself and those around you—like your partner, kids, or anyone you live with. Even if you live alone, small habits shape who you are.

Putting on fresh clothes each morning can set a positive tone for your day.

Simple routines can make a big difference: wake up a bit earlier, move your body, and get dressed for the day—even if you work from home. Stock markets open early, trends change quickly, and sometimes you need to make money decisions in minutes. If you sleep through the action, you might miss out.

Dating in the fast lane: why being ready matters. If you want to date a wealthy person, HVM (High Value Man), or HVW (High Value Woman), know that their plans can be last minute. You can't date someone with a busy life if you can't move quickly and be ready to go. When I dated my husband, a well-known singer, we often took last-minute trips for his shows. My favorite memory is his concert in Senegal; I joined him fast. I learned that being ready isn't about vanity—it's about being open to opportunities. *If you stay ready, you don't have to get ready, and you won't miss out on significant memories.*

Professionalism matters when you work from home. Working in pajamas isn't professional—people can tell from your posture, energy, and presence. Be ready for the camera: keep your hair neat, your face fresh, your top presentable, your background tidy, and the lights on. When a meeting link pops up or a client wants a quick video call, you shouldn't have to rush to clean up. Give yourself a daily reset so your space always looks good. *Professionalism shows, even on Zoom.*

Keep yourself professionally ready by constantly learning new skills and updating your knowledge. Upgrade your tools regularly to keep up with changes and take advantage of new opportunities. Read a page, watch a lesson, or practice a skill—being consistent is what matters. *Readiness is a habit, not a one-time thing.*

Be willing to learn outside your primary field. It can take years to find your true passion, and learning unique skills gives you more options and better experiences. Stay curious and keep exploring—new opportunities will appear. If you want to start a business, take action. Do your research and write a simple business plan to turn your idea into reality. *Keep your plan and key documents ready for any opportunities.* Most business grants aren't widely advertised—you might hear about them from a friend or a late-night message, and then the deadline is suddenly here. When that "apply now" moment comes, you don't want to send in a messy package. Keep your one-pager, financial pitch, and registrations up to date so your application always looks professional.

Your routines shape your reputation. Friends, family, partners, and investors all form opinions based on what they see. If your space is messy and your clothes look disorganized, people might doubt your reliability. Imagine giving your money to someone in wrinkled, dirty clothes—would you trust them? We trust bankers partly because they look neat and respectable. If you want the same trust, be ready and keep habits that show you are dependable.

S FOR SOCIALIZE

Socializing is a way to learn. When you connect with different people, beliefs, clubs, sports, or faith groups, you see new perspectives. Communities like churches can give you a sense of belonging, support, and structure, but they don't define someone's goodness.[110] Respect the different paths people choose. How you speak is important in social settings. The words you use, your tone, and your avoidance of profanity all shape how others see you. For example, in formal situations, choose words like "obtain" instead of "get." Your voice represents your brand, and your words make an impression before you even shake hands.[111]

Don't only stay at home. Go out and meet people face-to-face. This is a better way to build businesses and relationships. [112] Check city and state websites, Eventbrite, venue calendars, parks, and local theaters for free or paid events. Add these events to your calendar, attend them, and follow up afterward. Join or start a community. Spend time with people who are growing, such as those in industry groups, professional associations, or local businesses. Give your field the same focus you give other areas, and you'll see results.

Manage your calendar well: set reminders for important events, and send cards or messages for birthdays, holidays, and hospital visits. Keep your contact list organized and send personal greetings instead of generic ones. People remember thoughtful gestures.

Respect people's beliefs and cultures. Honoring your beliefs and respecting others' paths brings peace and a clear conscience. While disrespecting someone's faith can be hurtful, people's beliefs often come from different journeys. Some people are born into their beliefs, while others find them later in life. My father was a very spiritual person. He encouraged the whole family to go to church, even though he stayed home. I was always curious about why he was asking us to go to church while he wasn't. But he participated through donations and through prayer. However, I only understood his spirituality later because he was connected to several churches and to his ancestors as well. He stayed up late, meditated, prayed, and connected with ancestors. He practiced both spiritual traditions and Christianity, reciting psalms and living his faith every day. From him, I learned that spirituality could take many forms. I began putting the pieces together and understanding him better when I started my own spiritual journey.

As your network grows, you may wonder how to meet new and influential people. You can change your circle, habits, and environment with some effort, but how do you connect with wealthy individuals?

One way is to join exclusive, members-only clubs, such as the Union League Club, Metropolitan Club; Yale Club; Harvard Club; Bohemian Club; The Boule; The Links, Augusta National Golf Club; Royal and Ancient Golf Club of St Andrews; and the All-England Lawn Tennis and Croquet Club at Wimbledon. These clubs usually require an invitation, sponsorship, approval from current members, and a careful vetting process with high fees.[113] In these places, influential people connect, build trust, and share opportunities.

Another way to meet wealthy people is through higher education and elite schools. Attending an Ivy League university or a top private school, like The Lawrenceville School in New Jersey, gives you access to strong alumni networks and classmates from wealthy families. [114] If you've already graduated, this may not be an option for you, but it could be a good path for your children. With some research, you'll find many colleges and universities beyond the Ivy League where high-value people and their families are present. If you excel in your field, you may also connect with these circles through university events, lectures, and professional recognition.

Your neighborhood matters. Where you live affects who you meet every day. Spending time in wealthy areas can help you meet high-value people at local cafes, parks, or events. [115]

Attending significant networking events, first-class lounges, fundraising events, art auctions, galleries, well-known bars, exclusive nightclubs, or luxury venues is another good way to meet people. Activities that open doors to higher circles include learning to ride horses at equestrian events, playing golf at quality courses, taking swimming lessons at upscale hotels, and attending classical concerts, Broadway shows, or museum openings. These are places where people who value privacy, culture, and exclusivity gather.

Some jobs naturally connect you with wealthy people. For example, working as a waitress at a five-star restaurant, a sales associate at a high-end store, a personal dresser, a stylist, or an aesthetician in a luxury salon can give you more opportunities to meet affluent clients. Other jobs may not offer the same exposure or opportunities for growth in this area.[116]

The final best way to meet wealthy people is to become someone of value. Consider starting a business or offering a service that solves actual problems for affluent clients. When you have something valuable to offer, high-value people will be attracted to you. Work on improving your own life and values, and aim to contribute to the group rather than take from it. You can research where certain people spend time, but it's better to join their circles than to follow them. Make this a lifestyle, not a onetime effort. If this feels overwhelming, try spiritual coaching or seek trustworthy online advice. You won't meet high-value people by staying in your comfort zone. Build better habits, and your network will grow.

Information plays a big role: No matter who or what, know who the key people are. In your field and beyond, learn about important figures and stay updated so you can spot opportunities when they arise. Check sources like Forbes' lists to understand different industries and family businesses and see how they built lasting wealth. Many billionaires own companies, stocks, and public markets, which helps their businesses grow. They also share traits like vision and motivation. [117]

We can't talk about socializing without mentioning social media, which is one of the most powerful tools today.[118] It can help or hurt you, so use it wisely. Before posting, ask yourself if you'd be comfortable with your child, parent, grandparent, boss, or client seeing it. If yes, go ahead. Then, consider whether the post aligns with your goals. If it does, share it. Treat social media as your public portfolio. Show who you are and what you care about. Posting with intention, having a clear topic and consistent style helps the right people find you and builds genuine connections.[119]

Social media is important for everyone, and it's worth learning how to use it well.[120] Consider taking a class on social media, since it's now key to networking, building your image, and expanding your reach. Your page and online presence are crucial.[121] To keep up, follow new features, trending sounds, and weekly updates. Make it a habit to keep learning, since social media is always changing. If you are a parent, talk regularly with your children about how and when to use social media. Helping them build good habits early will help them use these platforms wisely and safely.

As I mentioned earlier, celebrations are some of the best ways to connect with others. Many of you have already planned parties, and if you've done it more than once, you're an organizer. Still, every event teaches you something new and brings surprises. There's always a moment when you notice a special detail or have an unexpected experience and think, "I want that at my next party." These moments show that parties let us step into a dream and create lasting memories. So, whether you're the guest of honor at a birthday, wedding, or shower, you shouldn't have to plan everything by yourself.

Share your ideas with a professional and let them help make your dream a reality so that you can enjoy the event without stress. Sometimes, involving friends and family adds extra pressure, and every event, big or small, has its own challenges. Working with an experienced planner lets you focus on what matters most, without worrying about the details. Planners know how to bring your vision to life, coordinate vendors, and handle last-minute issues so your event runs smoothly. They can also offer creative solutions and resources you might not have thought of, making even a modest budget go further while still creating a memorable experience.

If you decide to plan the event yourself, don't be afraid to keep things simple and focus on the secrets that make a celebration enjoyable. The secret to a grand party is always the same: the decorations, the DJ, and the food. You can't go wrong with these three.[122] As I mentioned, reach out to a professional who can help you host a memorable event even on a small budget. Regardless of what you decide, remember my three essentials: decoration, DJ, and food.

Building strong relationships and making a good impression starts with everyday habits.

Whether you connect in person or online, a few thoughtful practices can help you stand out, build trust, and grow a meaningful network.

Use these socializing tips to handle social situations with confidence and authenticity:

When you laugh out loud, cover your mouth to be polite.

Always bring something to a party.

Social media lets you show your true self and what matters to you. Use it thoughtfully.

Keep your online presence active by posting about your interests at least once a week or once a month.

Make eye contact, smile, and give a firm but friendly handshake.

Stay away from gossip and negative talk. Encourage others and keep your conversations positive.

Follow up after meeting someone new, even if it's a brief message.

Share credit and celebrate others' successes. Generosity builds trust.

Learn the basics of dining, networking, and even etiquette.

Be open to meeting people from different backgrounds and industries. Diversity strengthens your network.

Set boundaries. Quality connections matter more than quantity.

Practice gratitude and thank your host, organizers, or anyone who helps you connect.

Keep a backup phone so you don't lose communication when you need it.

Never pick your nose or scratch any part of your body when around people. Feel uncomfortable, take a restroom break.

Never leave the restroom without washing your hands. It shows a lack of cleanliness and is inconsiderate of others. Nobody wants to shake the hand of anyone who does not wash their hand.

Request the dress code each time you receive an invitation.

Ask for consent before you hug anyone.

Limit handshaking. In fact, never shake hands unless you are offered to do so.

Never enter a room without saying hello to the people who were in before you.

During events, please do not stick to people you know; greet them and go on to meet those you don't know.

T FOR THANK YOU

Thankful for each new day. Take a moment to feel grateful as soon as you wake up; it can set the tone for your whole day. Appreciating what you have and the people in your life helps you feel positive and content. Try to turn negative thoughts into uplifting ones and spend time with people who bring positive energy. These are the people you connect with and learn from, whether they are nearby or far away—friends, family, mentors, or peers. It's never too late to show gratitude. You can say it, write it, or show it through your actions. When you express gratitude, genuinely feel it.

I want to begin by thanking my late mother. Her lessons in etiquette and manners still shape who I am and how I interact with others. She showed actual class, lived honestly, and practiced gratitude every day. The best lessons are the ones we see lived, not taught.

I am, equally grateful to my late father. His encouragement and wisdom prepared me for life. He taught me how to live, but also how to "fish." By his example, he showed me the value of investing in different businesses. I'm still trying to reach the high standard he set, and his lessons were always given with love. I'm thankful for my late husband who loved me unconditionally, and the strength of his love gave me a true understanding of what love is at its core. Because of him, I know the difference between genuine love, and its imitation. His words and thoughts will stay with me forever.

I am also grateful to my son, who recently graduated with many honors, including Student of the Year and the Triple C Award from the Attorney General. His success as a student makes me proud.

Thank you to my family members who have always been there for me. Family is a genuine gift. I'm also grateful to my friends, especially those who have supported me through every season. Your calls, your presence, and your belief help me on tough days and make the good days even better. Loyalty is love in action.

A special thank you to my professors at BMCC (Borough of Manhattan Community College), Queens College, and SNHU (Southern New Hampshire University). You taught me, helped me grow, and opened new possibilities for me. Your guidance changed how I think and shaped my future. Influential teachers do more than teach; they inspire and transform.

I'm thankful for the teams at well-known magazines like Vogue, ELLE, Essence, and Cosmopolitan, and for the writers at Time, Vanity Fair, Harper's Bazaar, People, Rolling Stone, Billboard, and Life. Their creativity and hard work have shaped fashion media and left a lasting mark. As a teenager, I loved reading fashion magazines with my friends, cutting out photos and tips to put on my bedroom wall. Iman and Linda Evangelista were my favorite models. I read every line and caption, soaking up style and inspiration. Music was also an enormous influence: Janet Jackson and Anita Baker were on my first cassette tapes, and Halle Berry's talent and haircut inspired my own. I'm grateful for the music that shaped me, from the 80s to the 90s — Madonna, Chaka Khan, Lisa Lisa, Mary J. Blige, New Edition, Force M.D.'s, The Gap Band, The Police, Shalamar, Guy, Keith Sweat, TLC, NAS, Mariah Carey, Monica, and many more.

Big thank you to Wu-Tang Clan, who have supported Staten Island communities through their music and inspired younger generations to see further into the future.

Now it's your turn. Think of three people who helped you grow this year. Please send a thank-you message to one of them today. Gratitude grows when you share it. A simple note can brighten someone's day and yours. Also, take a moment to notice what you've gained this year that you didn't have before.

Being thankful is not limited to recognizing what you have. It's a new journey rooted in success and greater magnetism.

U FOR USING THE RIGHT TOOL

Using the right tool is essential for safety, demonstrating respect, and achieving optimal results. It is important to review instructions prior to beginning any task. Using the incorrect tool can cause wasted time, frustration, or injury. For instance, pouring hot coffee into a glass of water or using unsuitable screws during furniture assembly can lead to complications.[123] Matching the tool to the task prevents damage, conserves time, and maintains organization.[124] The right tool enables the highest-quality work.

This idea works online as well. Every social media platform and app has its own purpose. Choose the right one to reach your audience or meet your goal. If you use the wrong tool, your message might not work as well.

Home: Comfort, Cleanliness, and Organization

At home, using the right tools makes daily routines easier and more enjoyable. Start with your bed: use layers that fit the season, like a mattress protector, fitted and flat sheets, a quilt or duvet, and comfortable pillows. Wash your bedding often to stay healthy. [125] In the kitchen, pick the right tool for each job: a can opener for cans, a blender for purees, or a coffee maker for coffee.[126] Keep your closet tidy with sturdy hangers, drawer dividers, and bins for each season. Clean more easily with the right tools: microfiber cloths for dusting, a mop for floors, and a squeegee for windows. [127]

Setting the Table: How to Set a Table with Confidence

Acquiring the skill of setting a table is a valuable aspect of daily living. Practicing proper etiquette, maintaining organization, and attending to details contribute to a welcoming and comfortable dining experience, regardless of the occasion.

Begin by putting a clean tablecloth or placemats on the table to protect it and add some style. Place the dinner plates in the center of each setting. If you're serving more than one course, stack the plates and bowls on top of the dinner plate in the order you'll use them.

Arrange the utensils in the order you'll use them, starting from the outside and moving in. On the left, put the salad or starter fork farthest from the plate, then the dinner fork closer in. On the right, place the dinner knife with the blade facing the plate, then the soup spoon or fish knife. If you're serving dessert, put a dessert spoon or fork horizontally above the plate.[128]

Place the bread plate above the forks and set a butter knife across it. Put the glasses above the knives, with the water glass directly over the knife and the wine glasses to the right, in the order you'll use them. If you need a coffee or teacup and saucer, place them to the right of the spoons.[129]

Fold napkins neatly and put them on the dinner plate, under the forks, or use a napkin ring to decorate.[130] For everyday meals, use the main utensils, plate, glass, and napkin. For special occasions, you can add base plates (chargers), place cards, and a centerpiece with fresh flowers or candles to make the table feel more festive. [131]

A well-set table shows your guests that you care and want them to feel welcome. It also helps the meal go smoothly because everyone has what they need nearby and can follow along easily. The main point is to be thoughtful and organized. Setting the table is about making people comfortable, not following rules.

A cosmetic pouch is most useful when kept inside a sturdy day bag. For daily use, store your cosmetics in your handbag rather than in the pouch.[132]

Let Color and Details Send the Right Message

Colors and subtle details convey messages, which may be interpreted differently across cultures.[133] For instance, red roses typically symbolize love and respect, though their meaning may vary by cultural context.

Pink roses often symbolize appreciation or gratitude, but their meaning can vary from place to place.

Yellow roses might symbolize friendship, or in some cultures, they can convey apology and reconciliation. Always check what 'yellow' means locally, since it can have both positive and sensitive meanings.

Red and yellow roses together often suggest joy or celebration, but the meaning can change depending on the situation.[134]

Orange roses usually show enthusiasm or desire, and in many traditions, they stand for admiration and fascination.

Select a gift that honors the occasion rather than competing with expectations. When chosen with care, even something simple conveys genuine appreciation—a gift that says, I value you. I notice you. I thought of you. The same principle of intentional detail applies to how you dress.

Dressing: Matching the code and dressing the right way are other examples of using the right tool. In the past, you might have asked a friend how you looked. Now you can use the new Classy Check app (ClassyCheck.com) to double-check your outfit. For interviews, wear neat, well-fitting clothes, polished shoes, and a light scent. Adjust your daily outfit to your workplace, keep a blazer or sweater handy, and follow event dress codes. Accessories matter too: keep cosmetic pouches in your bag, and pick jewelry or watches that suit the occasion. Choose practical items for work, expressive ones for social events, and elegant pieces for formal settings. [135]

Communication: Words, Tone, and Medium

Selecting the communication mode ensures clarity and respect. Use email for formal correspondence, text messages for brief updates, and phone calls for urgent or sensitive matters.[136] Meetings are more effective with a prepared agenda and notes.[137] Provide feedback constructively and positively.[138] Incorporate slides or charts to enhance the clarity of presentations.[139]

Learning and Growth: Resources and Mentors

For personal development, selecting the resource—such as a book, course, mentor, or community—can significantly influence progress. Use language applications or classes for learning, and practice with native speakers.

Choose fitness programs, equipment, or trainers that align with individual needs. When encountering challenges, consult experts, mentors, coaches, groups, or forums. The right resources accelerate learning and growth.

Health and Well-being: Begin by identifying the specific health concern and determining the appropriate specialist, such as a psychologist. Avoid addressing serious issues like substance abuse or mental illness independently or solely with family support, as this may exacerbate the situation.[140] Instead, accurately assess the issue and consult the relevant professional. If uncertain, seek guidance and referrals from a primary care physician. Use fitness trackers to promote physical activity, drink water regularly to maintain hydration, and employ meal planners for balanced nutrition.[141] Engaging in mindfulness meditation or therapy journaling can help reduce stress and improve well-being.[142] Research has shown that practices like gratitude journaling can increase well-being and mental health.[143] For first aid, ensure access to essential supplies such as bandages, a thermometer, and emergency contact information.[144]

Money Management: Financial Tools and Habits

Managing your money is easier when you use the right tools. Try a budgeting app to track your spending, save, and invest. Open more than one account and use one with limited amount to set up automatic bill payments. For taxes, use reliable software or ask a professional for help. When shopping, use price comparison and coupon apps to save money. Consulting a financial advisor is the right tool and the best option for money management.

Relationships and Social Life: It's about using the right approach. It means picking what works best for each person and situation. Some people like encouraging words, others prefer quality time, and some value acts of service. Pay attention, listen, and adjust how you communicate and support others. The right gesture at the right time can make relationships stronger and help solve problems.

Giving and Community: Tools for Impact

To maximize impact, use effective tools for charitable giving. Consider donation platforms, volunteer matching services, or setting reminders to check on neighbors. Share expertise with organizations and facilitate connections to new opportunities within your network.

Core Principle: Details make the right choice. It keeps your message clear and effective. Details matter because they send messages.

The right tool shows respect and helps you succeed.

Overall, using the right tools applies to every area of life. For any situation, seek a qualified professional instead of spending hours discussing sensitive matters with people who may lack the expertise—or may later judge or criticize you. While it's natural to want to talk things through, be selective about whom you approach. We all possess unique skills, and sometimes the wisest choice is to acknowledge and rely on others' expertise. As you wouldn't use the wrong tool for an important task, seek the right professional for the challenges you face. Choose your tools and your advisors wisely.

V FOR VOLUNTEERING

Volunteering isn't about doing good—it can help you start your career, build new skills, and meet new people.[145] When you give your time, you gain perspective, confidence, and connections that can lead to new opportunities.[146] Service is a seed that can grow into something bigger later. Set an easy goal for yourself: volunteer a few hours each month in your community. Don't make excuses. Pick causes that matter to you, like schools, shelters, arts programs, senior centers, parks, health drives, or faith groups. Even small, regular efforts help your neighborhood grow stronger.

My parents always helped family, friends, and even strangers. When I was young, I didn't always get it, and sometimes I felt upset since some people seemed ungrateful. But as I grew older, I realized that giving isn't about getting thanks—it's about making the world better. Even when people don't notice, your kindness can bring rewards you don't expect.

Helping your community, especially those who need it most, is important to your success.[147] Don't see it as something to do only when you have extra time—make it a regular part of your life. For example, choose a place and commit to visiting or donating, like a local mosque, church, or even an online group, every Friday. As the Old Testament says in Deuteronomy 15:10: "God will bless the giver in all their works because of this act of generosity.[148]

New opportunities often arise when entrepreneurs start new businesses and need support. Volunteering your time with a new business can be both helpful and thoughtful. You can also get involved with local nonprofits, schools, faith groups, shelters, arts organizations, or small businesses that are getting started. After you volunteer, keep in touch with the people you meet—email, connect on LinkedIn, call, or follow up through the organization's website. These relationships can lead to new projects, recommendations, or even job offers.

Whenever you attend a volunteer or community event, introduce yourself and let people know you're willing to help and support new businesses. You can also mention on your resume that you're open to volunteer work or helping small businesses grow. Many employers appreciate this kind of initiative, and sometimes volunteer roles can turn into full-time jobs or promotions. [149] Volunteering isn't about giving back—it's a smart way to build your reputation, learn new skills, and find new opportunities.

There are many organizations to choose from, so pick one where you can give your time or skills. Helping more people move the mission forward faster. [150] If you can't give your time, give what you can—every bit makes a difference.

Donating money also helps. Think about giving monthly to a nonprofit you trust, but first check its mission, leadership, and impact. Give where your values match the results.

When you give with good intentions, both you and the person you help benefit. Serve to learn, make connections, and lift others up. Generosity leaves a lasting positive mark.

Your donations might be tax deductible, so keep your receipts and track your gifts. [151] Ask a tax professional for advice. Some employers have matching programs that can double your impact. [152]

W FOR WEALTHY

Wealth starts with how you think. Abundance comes from your beliefs, actions, and viewing failure as a learning tool. Perfection is subjective; it means perfection is different for each person, so focus on growth rather than comparison. Success results from small, steady habits.

Simple actions, like making your bed each morning or keeping your environment organized, signal your mind that you care about yourself and your goals. When you build these small habits, you reinforce your identity as someone who is committed to growth. Seek those who encourage your growth, celebrate their victories, and you'll find your own success speeding up. Celebrate others' wins to attract your own and remember that the love you give often comes back to you. The energy you put into the world—whether love, positivity, or support—returns, frequently multiplied.

What you focus on is what you attract.

Attraction and mindset are key to building wealth. The way you think and the habits you form shape what you bring into your life. When you focus on possibilities and gratitude, you see more opportunities. Your past doesn't define you—your choices and your willingness to change do. Even if the words aren't exact, the idea is clear. Gaining control over yourself means adjusting your mindset. You don't have to do this alone, and it's not always easy to figure out by reading books. Getting advice from a mentor or spiritual leader can be very helpful.

The key to wealth is discipline. You can have knowledge, talent, and opportunity, but without self-control, it's hard to build and keep anything. Spirituality can strengthen your discipline and mindset; both are foundational to building wealth. A clear sense of purpose and inner peace attracts opportunities and guides smart financial choices. The goal is to adopt a mindset that helps you turn your dreams into reality. You need real training and practice to get there.

Spirituality is a personal journey that helps you connect with yourself and the universe. It's about your values, your energy, and your growth. Spiritual people often understand religious and cultural practices deeply.[153] While religion is more about shared beliefs, practices, and traditions within a community. Both can be meaningful, but spirituality focuses more on personal change and finding meaning beyond rules. The aim is to raise your mindset, whether you use spiritual wisdom, religious practice, or both.

If you keep doing the same things, you'll keep getting the same results. Even good routines can hold you back if you never question them. To make fundamental changes, change your habits, which sometimes means stepping out of your comfort zone and trying something new.

Carl Jung is often linked to the idea, "Where your fear is, there is your task."[154] Even if the words aren't exact, the meaning is important: fear and growth go hand in hand.[155] Fear isn't a reason to stop; it shows you where you need to grow. *Absolute confidence is quiet and comes from steady progress and trusting yourself, while insecurity is loud.* When fear knocks, it tries to create a full stop where you need a bridge. *Don't let fear control you—use it to guide your next step.* Life is full of challenges and lessons. Facing what's hard helps you grow stronger and wiser.

The truth is, if you live without any fear, you may find it challenging to move to the next step. Sometimes, having a sense of respect or concern for at least one person—or one figure—can help you move forward. Put simply: if you don't have anyone you look up to or feel accountable to, it can be harder to find motivation to improve or challenge yourself.

That person could be a parent. I was afraid of my father, so I made sure I did what he said—simple, no questions. He told me, "Stop modeling," so I stopped. He told me, "Go and complete your education," and I did.

If there is nobody you particularly fear, consider looking around you and identifying someone you want to be loyal and faithful to. This can be very valuable in the long run. People who say they are not afraid of anybody may express it with confidence, but deep down, it is common to feel some level of vulnerability or connection to others.

Let's be clear: exclude those who do not add value to your life and focus on those who inspire you to be a better person—to learn, to grow, and to become your best.

Learning never stops. Stay curious and open-minded. Find what genuinely interests you, learn more about it, and don't be afraid to ask for help. Share your journey with people who support and challenge you. Keep your thoughts organized, set clear goals, and focus on finding solutions instead of seeing problems. Progress isn't always a straight line. Some days will be tough, but every setback can help you come back even stronger.

Act → Fail → Learn → adjust → Iterate → Succeed.

This is a powerful way to grow. Every failure teaches you something; every lesson helps you make changes, and each change brings you closer to your goals.

Wealth, in every sense, starts from within. It's about who you are, how you think, and the energy you give to others. Begin today by changing your mindset, improving your habits, and choosing your influences wisely. The journey never truly ends, but every step you take brings you closer to a richer, more fulfilling life.

When my son was in 4th grade, his teacher assigned us a family project: to create a display of everything we wanted as a family. He picked a toboggan and his favorite toys, and I added a luxury car with a TV. We made a collage. After his teacher checked the project, he brought it home, and we hung it on our dining room wall. Then we put it away, and we didn't talk about it again. Two years later, I realized that everything we wished for in that collage had come true—my son had his toboggan and toys, and I was driving a luxury car with a TV. Often, what you truly want finds its way to you, especially if you keep your vision clear. I learned that vision plus effort equals "good luck." That's what helps you reach your dreams. Now take a moment to think about these two questions: What is my dream? What do I want? Draw a picture of your answers and keep it for yourself. If you haven't found your vision yet, you can get a free analysis profile at GeneKey.com to explore your life's work and purpose with excitement.

As Dolores Cannon stated: "If you can visualize it in your mind, it must happen; that's a law of the universe." She also explained, "What is it that you want in your life? Write it down so that, if you were to visualize it, you could see it, hear it, smell it."[156] The more detail you can put in, the easier it is for the universe to know what you want." That means it is extremely important to at least know what you want; we cannot complain about not having it while we cannot dictate our minds. I knew nothing about Cannon's philosophy when I did my son's homework. But later, I came to deeply understand the importance of keeping clear goals.

In addition, being part of a group or association can help you grow, as I shared in S for Socialize. Pick one thing to do today—join a group, start a conversation, or explore something new. Act now to shape your path. When you focus your actions on a clear goal, you can achieve almost anything.

Here is a list of different income you can explore and start building:

Renting out storage space or parking spots

Affiliate marketing

Print-on-demand merchandise (t-shirts, mugs, etc.)

YouTube or podcast ad revenue

Voice-over for commercial and movie translation

Cashback and rewards programs

Dividend-paying ETFs and index funds

Licensing your photography or artwork online

Stocks: Begin by making small, regular purchases, like buying one share or a set amount each month. Over time, your investments can grow and split, and dividends can add up. It's never too late to get started.

Real estate: Owning property can build long-term value and, if managed well, can even pay for itself. Talk to a real estate expert to look at your options, financing, and the local market.

Write eBooks or audiobooks.

Build a blog and monetize high-value topics.

Sell digital products or templates.

Develop an app or tool.

Place and manage ATMs in the right locations

Invent a helpful product.

Buy a profitable business with seller financing.

Note: Before pursuing any of these income streams, consult with a financial advisor or a professional experienced in that specific field for personalized advice and guidance.

Starting or growing a business can seem impossible if you don't have money. If that's your situation, don't wait for luck. Waiting for fortune can leave you waiting forever. Make your own opportunities by taking action and improving your approach as you go. Start small and build a solid foundation. Don't wait for the perfect time or a lot of money. Begin with what you have and grow from there. Don't be afraid to start small.

 The truth is simple: if you have nothing to sell, you can't complain about not making money. It's your job to create something of value and put it on the market. Choose something you have experience in—something you know well—or something you genuinely feel passionate about.

Shakespeare wrote in King Lear (Act 1, scene 1) "Nothing will come of nothing," a principle that applies equally to building wealth: you must start with something to create something. Without money, you cannot make money. The same way a farmer needs seeds to plant, most businesses need money to start. You could also consider getting a business loan. These are often easier to qualify for than personal loans. Talk to your bank or private lender about the requirements and compare the terms before you apply. Another good option is to apply for a grant, since you don't have to pay it back. Both lenders and grant programs want to see a powerful story, and a solid plan, so how you present yourself matters. You can write your own applications or hire a professional grant writer. Even small grants can help you get started.

If you're looking for personal growth instead of funding, there are resources to help. For women who want finishing-school-style training, etiquette and schools like Emma Dupont Etiquette School in London[157] and other places offer lessons in social skills, confidence, and presence. These programs can help you build the confidence to succeed anywhere. Put yourself in environments where your goals can grow—choose communities and events that match your aims. The people and places you choose can shape your results. Never neglect these three faiths: God, the universe, and your roots.

X FOR XOXO

XOXO, or hugs and kisses, stand for affection, tenderness, and care. There are many types of hugs—like family hugs, self-hugs, bear hugs, and more—many kinds of kisses, such as forehead, cheek, hand, butterfly, peck, French, nose and air kisses. There are endless ways to say and show "love," whether it's through gifts, quality time, kind words, helpful actions, or touch. What matters most is how you like to give and receive love, and how you share that with your partner.

Ancient Greeks identified eight types of love, but we can simplify to two major categories: unconditional love and agreement-based (or contractual) love.[158] Know which one you practice and be honest about what it means. In every partnership, people want to work together—whether it's raising kids, running a home, building a business, or finding peace. Communication is the key. Good communication keeps relationships healthy.

Without it, minor issues can grow; with it, you can work through differences together.[159]

Unconditional love doesn't mean unspoken expectations. Even when love feels limitless, you still need structure: shared goals, money plans, time boundaries, household roles, faith or cultural practices, family expectations, and personal space.[160]

People change all the time, and your partner might change for many reasons. As Hermann Hesse said, "Some of us think holding on makes us strong, but sometimes it is letting go." [161] Sometimes, letting go is the best choice; allowing your partner to find happiness elsewhere can show genuine love. Lasting love needs both honesty and flexibility.

To see if someone truly loves you, watch how they act when you stop doing what you usually do. This slight change can help you spot real affection.[162] Love needs both warmth and clear understanding.

A classy person must understand emotional intelligence—and practice it daily by managing emotions with maturity and showing discernment in his or her love life and in the workplace. Emotional intelligence helps you communicate clearly, set boundaries, and avoid unnecessary conflict. When you master your emotions, you protect your reputation, your relationships, and your peace.

It's normal to feel hurt, angry, disappointed, or overwhelmed. But your behavior is your responsibility—meaning you are still accountable for what you say and do, even when emotions are strong. Emotional intelligence is pausing before you react, choosing respectful words, and handling conflict with self-control instead of impulse.

In addition, some people benefit from therapy to strengthen emotional intelligence—especially if former experiences, anxiety, depression, trauma, or repeated relationship patterns make self-control and communication harder. If that is your case, start therapy with a **licensed mental health professional** (such as a psychologist, licensed clinical social worker, mental health counselor, or marriage and family therapist). Common approaches include **Cognitive-Behavioral Therapy (CBT)** for thoughts and reactions, **Dialectical Behavior Therapy (DBT)** for emotional regulation and communication skills, and **trauma-informed therapy** when past pain is still affecting the present.

The goal is not perfection—it's progress. With support and consistent practice, you can become emotionally ready for a healthy relationship.

Looking for love? Choose your path carefully. Whether you use matchmakers, relationship coaches (even those for public figures or "high-value men"), or dating apps, remember each option has its own pros and cons. Curated introductions can be expensive but selective, while apps give you more choices but can bring more noise and risk.[163] Whatever you choose, use moral judgment. Check reputations, protect your privacy, and set healthy boundaries. Focus on what truly fits you, not what's popular online. If you want a wealthy partner, make sure you're in a similar place at your own level or work on improving your life first. [164] Start relationships without extra baggage and stay hopeful: while "Cinderella" stories are nice, today's world values substance as much as looks. [165]

Don't commit to marriage or living together without clear, agreed-upon goals. Remember, being single isn't a failure—it's a choice. If you feel fulfilled and your needs are met, marriage is an option, not a must. Always choose a **partnership** because you want to, not because you feel pressured. You're the one who lives with your choices.

Affection without clear agreements can be confusing, and agreements without affection can feel cold.

<u>Example Relationship Agreement Template 1: Cohabiting Couples</u>

Intent and values we commit to: Mutual respect, honesty, and building a life of mutual purpose, supporting each other.

Communication rules: Use a respectful voice; pause and resume within 2 hours; hold weekly updates on Sunday evenings.

Conflict resolution: Acknowledge, apologize, ask "What do you need?" and make one change. No breakup threats. If the same issue keeps coming up, talk about what isn't working and adjust the agreement together. If a problem happens several times and feels hard to solve, consider getting outside support, like counseling, or review the agreement with help so both people feel supported.

Time and attention: Daily phone-free time (30 minutes); date night weekly; alone time (2 hours/week); and Shared calendar.

Money: Budget by category; spend limit without check-in ($150); savings goal (10% monthly).

Home roles and cleanliness: Cooking alternates; cleaning is split by room; baseline standard is always Guest-ready.

Family/faith/culture: Holidays rotate among families; relatives visit with 48 hours' notice; Sunday faith practices are honored.

Phones/social: Ask before posting; DMs stay respectful; passwords remain private unless mutually agreed.

Intimacy/health: Open communication on definitions, testing cadence, contraception decisions, and substance boundaries. To help start these conversations, you could ask, "What does intimacy mean to you?" or "How often should we check in about our sexual health or set up testing?" You might also say, "How can we make sure we both feel safe and comfortable?" or "Are there any boundaries or preferences you'd like to share?"

Safety: Zero tolerance for violence, threats, stalking, or financial sabotage.

Review cycle: Every 6 months; exit with dignity if needed.

Keep things simple and easy to understand. If you want to share this agreement with your partner, you could start with a gentle question like, "Would you like to try this together?" or "What do you think about making an agreement like this for us?" This helps both people feel more comfortable and open to the idea.

Example Relationship Agreement Template 2: Dating Couples

Intent and values we commit to: Kindness, consistency, and honest communication.

Intent: Exclusive and long-term focused.

Communication: Preferred channels: phone and text; response window: 3 hours; weekly check-in: Wednesday evenings.

Time: Date weekly; 24-hour notice for cancellations; overnight stays by mutual agreement only.

Boundaries and safety: Open conversation on health testing, contraception, and substance boundaries. Zero tolerance for violence, threats, stalking.

Money/gifts: Alternate treating; celebrate birthdays and anniversaries.

Social media: Ask before posting private moments; DMs stay respectful; passwords remain private.

Friends/family: Introductions after 3 months; PDA at each person's comfort level.

Review: Revisit every 6 months; part with respect if needed.

Use these agreements as a starting point and adjust the details to match your life and values. For example, couples with young children might set an earlier phone-free time to fit kids' bedtimes or change check-in days to work around parenting. If you work different shifts, you can swap check-in days or choose times when you are both in the house.

You can agree on flexible standards for chores or rest time that suit everyone. The main idea is to shape the agreement around your routines and priorities. When big life changes happen, like illness, moving, or job loss, it helps to revisit your agreement together, so it still fits your situation. Updating your agreement during these times shows both of you that it can change as your lives change.

To help guide your review, consider the following questions:

What is working well for us right now?

Are there any parts of our agreement that feel challenging?

Has anything changed in our lives or routines that we should address?

What do we appreciate about each other or our partnership?

Is there anything we want to add, remove, or adjust in this agreement?

These prompts can support an honest and productive conversation during your review.

Sincerity and Red Flags (Protect Your Peace). If someone avoids being clear about basics like money, respect, safety, or privacy, or turns slight issues into enormous problems, take that as a warning sign. Making them "a friend" won't change their behavior, so protect your boundaries. People who pick fights over small things to distract from actual issues are playing games. Don't chase after chaos. You are valuable, and you stay valuable with the right person who supports you. Don't compare yourself to others; every couple is unique.

Important Conversation Starters

What does "us on a normal Tuesday," look like?

How do we handle money, chores, holidays, and in-laws?

Phones and privacy: what's okay, what's not?

How do we repair after conflict—and how quickly?

What does intimacy mean to each of us?

Y FOR YOUTHFUL

Youthfulness is more than age. It's a mindset that spreads positivity and encouragement. We need people with great energy, warm smiles, uplifting words, and a motivating presence—and we should aim to be that person too. If you want youthful energy around you, bring it with you. Let's stay young and motivated.

Being youthful means feeling young, strong, and happy. Life has its difficulties, but our job is to rise, reset, and keep living fully. Enjoy simple pleasures like fresh air, sunlight on your face, clean sheets, or a quiet walk. These small joys show that life is still generous.

This is only the start of genuine happiness. In another book, I'll share personal stories about cravings, challenges, and how I worked through them. For now, remember this: things often happen for a reason, even if the lesson comes later. Finding meaning can turn setbacks into steps forward.

Some people get hard news and still transform it through practice. Meditation, prayer, and breath-work help create a calm space within where emotions can settle, and wisdom can emerge. It's like training your nervous system for peace. There are many helpful videos online, but the most important thing is to clear your mind of negative thoughts so youthful enthusiasm can thrive.

A quiet mind helps you have a bright spirit.

Youthfulness also shows on the outside, but it starts from within. Stay in shape by eating healthy food, moving regularly, and getting good sleep. Choose a sport you enjoy and add a simple routine you can stick to. Treat your workouts, meals, and bedtime like important appointments.

Discipline is a way to show self-love.

Put your health first. Learn what helps your body and what doesn't and adjust as needed. Drinking water, eating colorful whole foods, getting enough protein, stretching, and having regular checkups all help you stay young. Try to limit things that drain you, like too much sugar, ongoing stress, or endless scrolling on your phone. Protect your energy as you protect your time.

Let's talk about Generation X, a group known for being revolutionary and for embracing youthfulness and adaptability at any age. For them, aging is more about mindset than years. Generation X and Millennials (Generation Y) are modern, adaptable, and always up to date with trends, technology, and information.166 Whether it's pop culture, digital innovation, or new ideas, they adapt quickly and offer fresh insights. Their mix of experience and a forward-looking attitude makes them stand out in today's changing world.

Today, people in their 40s, 50s, and 60s approach aging differently from how people did decades ago. The "new" 30 to 70 looks and feels younger than ever. Instead of keeping up, this generation is redefining what it means to grow older. They show that age is only a number when you have curiosity, energy, and a modern mindset.

There are now many cosmetic procedures and tools to help us stay youthful, far beyond Botox and facials. Popular options include microdermabrasion, chemical peels, laser skin resurfacing, dermal fillers, microneedling, and radiofrequency skin tightening. There are also many anti-aging creams and serums. It's an actual change—there are no more excuses to look or feel old if you don't want to. Youthfulness is a choice you make. Breathe, believe, move, and smile, then share that light with others.

Live stress-free and flourish every moment with a classy mindset by refreshing your mind. A simple way to refresh your mindset in the morning is to take one minute for deep breathing and write one sentence of gratitude. The deep breathing technique should be done many more times than once a day. In the evening, write one thing and one lesson from your day. Live stress-free by spending more time with people who lift you up and eliminate or limit time with those who drain you.

Having fun doing what you love: playing games, dancing, socializing, learning. "Anyone who stops learning is old, whether at twenty or eighty. Anyone who keeps learning stays young. The greatest thing in life is to keep your mind young," 167 That means using your time on the right activities to stay young. Note that "We don't stop playing because we grow old; we grow old because we stop playing."168

Z FOR ZONE

Zone matters: protect your peace by choosing people, places, and habits that support you. A classy life is about choosing values, goals, and positive energy over busyness or overwhelm. The company you keep shapes your mood—choose those who brighten your world.

Life happens for a reason, especially when staying in your zone. My experience as a psychic reader deepened my understanding of the symbolism of playing cards. A standard deck has 52 cards, divided into two perfect halves: 26 red cards and 26 black cards.[169] The deck only works because both halves are complete and equal. Remove one half and the game cannot be played. This is the nature of balance.

 Treat your year like a deck of cards: each week, season, and month offers its own lessons. Identify your current "suit," recognize your energy and strengths, and stay open to surprises. Focus on present strengths and align with your timing to set your space and make thoughtful choices.

When you receive an invitation, act as the **Jack**—a symbol of curiosity and new beginnings. Be open, interested, and thoughtful. Ask questions, observe, and collect information before deciding. Move forward with care and curiosity, not haste. Let hope guide you, but do not rush your choices. For more context, check public profiles or talk to mutual friends.

Channel the **Queen** when choosing who belongs in your space. Use wisdom, warmth, and moral judgment. Like the Queen selecting her court, you shape an environment that supports rather than drains you. Every interaction reveals who shares your values. Balance warmth with clear standards so your space can thrive. Lead with purpose, and both your confidence and others' confidence will grow.

Step into the **King** when choosing places that match your style and set the right mood. The King chooses his space with care and confidence, so look beyond the address and consider the atmosphere, rules, and whether the place aligns with your values. Before you go to a restaurant, club, gallery, or event, do your research: check reviews, menus, and dress codes, and get a sense of the crowd. Preparation helps you enter spaces that match your standards—and it lets your confidence and elegance show.

A classy person uses the wisdom of the court cards, choosing where to go with intention instead of going anywhere. Even if you are invited, check things for yourself. Arrive prepared, ready to enjoy yourself, and ready to show your best side. This is the spirit of the **Ace**: start each meeting with purpose. Being ready ahead of time shows true confidence—before you even walk in.

Know your emotions—your inner zone. Psychologist Paul Ekman identified universal feelings: joy, sadness, fear, disgust, anger, and sometimes surprise.[170] These core emotions are ingrained and guide decisions. Therapy Hub notes that they send signals through interactions, shaping self-understanding and well-being.[171] As a classy person, recognize what triggers you, choose your response, and disengage from the unnecessary. Name your feeling, then decide what to do next.

The "sport zone" is a good example: athletes talk about being "in the zone"—calm, focused, and present, with enough challenge to feel alive. You can do this in life too: cut out distractions, take a breath, set a clear goal, and match your effort to what's needed. In yoga, it's called Drishti (steady gaze); in running, it's rhythm; in dance, it's musicality. These are different words for the same feeling. Being present helps you do your best in any area.[172]

Remember, your zone is your responsibility. Choose your environment, protect your peace, and let your standards show through your actions.

Protecting your zone is an art, just like playing the right cards at the right time. Be the **Queen** when choosing people: pick your company with respect and avoid drama with grace. Be the King when picking places. Check the dress code, safety, and atmosphere, and always come and go on your own terms. Use Ace's clarity by leaving time buffers and not overbooking, so you can give your best to each moment. With technology, same as **Jack**—be curious but intentional—by silencing distractions and putting your phone away after you capture what matters. Finally, show the completeness of the **Ten** in your self-care: take a breath before you speak, smile as you enter, and say thank you as you leave, making sure every interaction starts and ends with grace.

The Number That Has Always Been Here.

Before we continue, there is something you should know about this chapter. You have just completed the 26th and final chapter of this book. The alphabet has 26 letters. This book has 26 chapters. And you are reading it in 2026. And that is not where the connections end.

The calendar mirrors the deck in surprising ways: Each year has 52 weeks. Week 26 is the exact midpoint—the halfway point of the year.[173] In business, week 26 is when companies review annual goals and decide what the second half will require. In sports, halftime is the moment the team reassesses and chooses how to play differently. Week 26 is the year's built-in reset: a moment to look at what the first half built and decide intentionally what the second half will become.

The Latin alphabet—the system that organizes written knowledge in the Western world—has exactly 26 letters.[174] Every word ever written in English is built from these 26. Nothing more is needed. Nothing is missing. This book uses all of them, A through Z. A complete system.

In gematria—an ancient numerical system used by Greek, Hebrew, and other scholars for thousands of years—each letter carries a numerical value: A equals 1, B equals 2, and so on through to Z, which equals 26.[175] Every name, every word, every title converts into a number rooted in this system.

In mathematics, 26 holds a position that no other number shares.[176] It is the only integer that sits between a perfect square and a perfect cube: 5 squared equals 25, and 3 cubed equals 27. Between those two powers sits 26—alone.

Your foot has 26 bones.[177] The foundation that carries you forward through every room, every challenge, and every chapter of your life is built on 26.

The sympathetic nervous system—the network inside your body that controls alertness, stress response, and survival—runs on 26 ganglions.[178] Class is not just how you dress or speak. It is how you respond under pressure.

On the periodic table, iron is element 26.[179] Iron is what makes your blood red. It is the molecule inside hemoglobin that carries oxygen from your lungs to every cell in your body.

In Jewish tradition, the divine name of God—written as YHWH—has a numerical value of 26: Yod (10) + Hey (5) + Vav (6) + Hey (5).[180]

The Hebrew word *kavod*—glory, weight, divine presence—is also said to equal 26 numerically.[181]

From Adam to Moses at the burning bush, there are said to be 26 generations.[182]

According to some scholars and historians, Jesus Christ began his public ministry in AD 26.[183]

In bosonic string theory, scientists propose that the full structure of the universe requires 26 space-time dimensions.[184]

The maximum time difference between any two points on Earth is 26 hours.[185]

Walt Disney won 26 Academy Awards—more than any individual in the history of the awards.[186]

From any configuration, a Rubik's Cube can be solved in 26 moves or fewer.[187]

The 26th Amendment to the United States Constitution gave 18-year-olds the right to vote.[188]

July 4, 2026, marks the 250th anniversary of the signing of the Declaration of Independence.[189]

26 is also connected to how we get paid in the USA. Many employers (including big businesses and city/state government) choose biweekly pay (every 2 weeks) since it matches the familiar 26-pay-period rhythm most workers recognize. Payroll operations are cheaper and simpler, with 26 payroll runs per year (not 52) reducing processing, approvals, corrections, and error risk at scale. It fits hourly work + overtime rules cleanly, by standardizing timecards, overtime, shift differentials, and union rules across mixed workforces on one schedule. Employees still feel it's frequent, with a steady 14-day rhythm. It supports while giving payroll teams time to reconcile hours and adjustments, it's consistent on the calendar, since it lands on the same weekday and avoids uneven gaps common in semi-monthly setups. Budgeting + cash-flow planning, allowing large

organizations to forecast payroll expenses more reliably. It standardizes practices across departments and agencies, Important detail: sometimes it's 27 paychecks, since 26 biweekly periods cover 364 days, and some calendar years create a 27th payday that payroll and budgets must account for in advance.[190]

In the plant world, taro has been documented to have chromosome counts of 2n = 26 among its varieties.[191]

The antlion has documented chromosome numbers reaching 2n = 26 in certain species of the Palparinae subfamily.[192]

Numbers are not just a count. They are a definition. They are a calculation. They appear in the structure of everything around us—in the alphabet that carries language, in the bones that carry your body, in the blood that carries your life, in the cards that map your year, in the weeks that hold your time, in the ancient name of the divine, in the genetic code of the oldest plants on earth, and in the year this book arrived in the world.

Some of these connections come to us unexpectedly. We did not choose that iron would be the 26th element. We did not choose that the foot would have 26 bones. We did not choose that the divine name in the oldest recorded spiritual tradition would equal 26. These things simply are—and they have always been—waiting to be noticed.

Some connections come by choice. You chose to read this book. You chose to reach Z. You chose to finish what you started.

And now—a question for you? When you see a number repeating in your life—your birth date, the number of letters in your name, the address where you built something meaningful, the year something finally arrived after delay after delay—do you see it as a coincidence? Or do you see it as a sign? The decision is yours.

There is one more thing you should know. 2 + 6 = 8. In the language of numbers, 8 is the universal signature of abundance, prosperity, and return—the only number whose symbol, turned on its side, becomes infinity: ∞ a loop that never ends. [193] Across cultures, 8 has always been the number of wealth, cycles, and what comes back to those who stay aligned.[194] You were never just reading a book about class and elegance. You were holding a number that carried the energy of abundance. That was not an accident.

Watch your numbers. Not with obsession—but with awareness. Numbers are not just a count. They carry history. They carry meaning. They carry the weight of things written long before you arrived.

This book has 26 chapters. You are holding it in 2026. And Z—the last letter, the final chapter, the place where you protect everything you have built—is where you were always meant to land.

Remember, your zone is your responsibility. Choose your environment, protect your peace, and let your standards show through your actions.

Your zone. Your number. Your alert. Your awakening. Your lifetime."
— Berthille Metoua

AUTHOR'S NOTE

"If you came this far.
That was never an accident.
Reset.
What happens next is entirely in your
hands."

- Berthille Metoua

CLASSY CHECK APP

Scan The Classy Check app by Berthille
Metoua QR Code

https://classycheck.com

UPCOMING BOOKS

The ABCs of Classy was just the beginning. It introduced you to 26 principles- one for every letter –
The next Upcoming Books by Berthille Metoua

Book One: Appropriateness

Book Two: Beauty

Book Three: Classy

Children's Books Collection (Nesse & Galia)
- Book 1: *Galia Wants to Know Everything*
- Book 2: *Nesse's Hidden Secrets*
- Book 3: *Galia's Dream*
- Book 4: *Nesse's Lesson*
- Book 5: *Christmas in the Jungle*

REFERENCES

A FOR APPROPRIATENESS
1 Aghaei, M., Parezzan, F., Dimiccoli, M., Radeva, P., & Cristani, M. (2017). Clothing and people – A social signal processing perspective. arXiv:1704.02231. https://doi.org/10.48550/arXiv.1704.02231
2 Bicchieri, C. (2025). Social norms, social change I. Coursera. https://www.coursera.org/learn/norms
3- Uno. (2024). The psychology of fashion and self-expression. BULB. https://www.bulbapp.io/p/914c3b27-abcd-4189-a3d3-80bddd3c0493/the-psychology-of-fashion-and-self-expression
4- Snyder, C. (2025). The mindful home: Creating your personal space for mental health. Healthline. https://www.healthline.com/health/creating-your-personal-space-for-mental-health
5- Dong, M., Zhou, D., Ma, J., & Zhang, H. (2025). Towards intelligent design. arXiv:2501.13396. https://doi.org/10.48550/arXiv.2501.13396
6- World Book Encyclopedia. (2025). Dress codes. Britannica ProCon. https://www.britannica.com/procon/dress-codes-debate
7- Peluchette, J. V., Karl, K., & Rust, K. G. (2006). Dressing to impress: Beliefs and attitudes regarding workplace attire. Journal of Business and Psychology, 21(1), 45–63. https://doi.org/10.1007/s10869-005-9022-1
8- Bae, H., & Kim, M. (2022). Everyday creativity practiced through a capsule wardrobe. Sustainability, 14(4). https://doi.org/10.3390/su14042092
9- Brescia, G. (2020). Change your clothes, change your life. Gallery Books
10- Jinnah, S. (2023). Dressing for respect: Cultural norms and attire. Journal of Cross-Cultural Studies.
11 -Zhang, X., Li, Y., & Wang, Z. (2024). Cultural dress codes and global etiquette. International Journal of Intercultural Relations

REFERENCES

12- PERCEPTIONS OF ETHICALITY: THE ROLE OF ATTIRE STYLE, ATTIRE APPROPRIATENESS, AND CONTEXT. (2023). JOURNAL OF BUSINESS ETHICS. HTTPS://DOI.ORG/10.1007/S10551-023-05156-0

13- ADAM, H., & GALINSKY, A. D. (2012). ENCLOTHED COGNITION. JOURNAL OF EXPERIMENTAL SOCIAL PSYCHOLOGY, 48(4), 918–925. HTTPS://DOI.ORG/10.1016/J.JESP.2012.02.008

14- DRESS TO IMPRESS: PUBLIC PERCEPTION OF PLASTIC SURGEON ATTIRE. (2021). AESTHETIC SURGERY JOURNAL. HTTPS://DOI.ORG/10.1093/ASJ/SJAB408

15- HOOKER, J. (2008). CULTURAL DIFFERENCES IN BUSINESS COMMUNICATION. IN H. KOTTHOFF & H. SPENCER-OATEY (EDS.), INTERCULTURAL DISCOURSE AND COMMUNICATION (PP. 389–407). WILEY-BLACKWELL.

16- GLOBAL COMPETENCY IMPACT OF SUSTAINED REMOTE INTERNATIONAL ENGAGEMENT FOR STUDENTS. (2023). BMC MEDICAL EDUCATION, 23. HTTPS://DOI.ORG/10.1186/S12909-023-04333-X

17 -MATERA, C., NERINI, A., & STEFANILE, C. (2018). WHY ARE MEN INTERESTED IN COSMETIC SURGERY PROCEDURES? BODY IMAGE, 26, 74–77. HTTPS://DOI.ORG/10.1016/J.BODYIM.2018.06.003

B FOR BEAUTY

18-Shekhawat, K. (2024). The psychological effects of makeup: Self-perception, confidence, and social interaction. International Journal of Advanced Research, 12(5), 925–931. https://www.journalijar.com/article/48616/the-psychological-effects-of-makeup-:-self-perception,-confidence-and-social-interaction/

[19]American Academy of Dermatology Association. (2025, September 8). *Gel manicures: Tips for healthy nails.* https://www.aad.org/public/everyday-care/nail-care-secrets/basics/pedicures/gel-manicures

[20]Wang, Z. (2023). The association between psychological factors and self-care in patients with heart failure: An integrative review. *European Journal of Cardiovascular Nursing, 22*(6), 553–561. https://doi.org/10.1093/eurjcn/zvad043

[21] Moji Nail Spa. (n.d.). *Why hands and nails are crucial for first impressions: A complete care guide.* https://mojiinailspa.com/article/detail/Why%20Hands%20and%20Nails%20Are%20Crucial%20for%20First%20Impressions%20A%20Complete%20Care%20Guide

REFERENCES

---

[22]Samer Khouzami. (2025). *Makeup for different face shapes: Enhance your features with precision.* https://www.samerkhouzami.com/blogs/makeup/makeup-for-different-face-shapes-enhance-your-features-with-precision

[23]Body water percentage: Average, ideal, how to maintain and determine. (2023). *Healthline.* https://www.healthline.com/health/body-water-percentage

[24]National Institutes of Health. (2023, January 19). *Good hydration can promote healthy aging. NIH Record.* https://nihrecord.nih.gov/2023/01/20/good-hydration-can-promote-healthy-aging

[25] Royston, J. (2020, August 10). Meghan Markle gave Prince Harry the confidence to quit royal family, author says. *Newsweek.* https://www.newsweek.com/meghan-markle-gave-prince-harry-confidence-quit-royal-family-author-says-1524579

C FOR CLASSY

[26] Jewelerloom. (2025). *The importance of pearl jewelry: An in-depth study.* https://jewelerloom.com/articles/importance-of-pearl-jewelry/

[27] The Emily Post Institute. (2023). Top table manners tips. https://emilypost.substack.com [Covers bread and butter rules, soup spoon direction, passing dishes, and the utensil "finished" signal.]

[28] The Emily Post Institute. (2024). Dining etiquette. https://emilypost.com/advice/dining-etiquette [Covers the 4 o'clock utensil signal for "finished," napkin protocol, toasting, and excusing yourself from the table.]

[29] von Drachenfels, S. (2000). The Art of the Table. Simon & Schuster. [The definitive illustrated reference on formal table setting, silverware, the BMW rule, and proper service — over 440 pages.]

[30] Tower, J. (2016). Table Manners: How to Behave in the Modern World and Why Bother. Farrar, Straus and Giroux. [A James Beard Award-winning chef's authoritative guide covering restaurant signals, check etiquette, hosting, and conversation rules.]

[31] Black, R. (2014). Dining Etiquette: Essential Guide for Table Manners, Business Meals, Sushi, Wine and Tea Etiquette. Etiquette Now! [Covers restaurant protocol, how to handle the menu, tipping, and cultural dining contexts.]

[32] von Drachenfels, S. (2000). The Art of the Table. Simon & Schuster. [The definitive illustrated reference on formal table setting, silverware, the BMW rule, and proper service — over 440 pages.]

REFERENCES

33 The Emily Post Institute. (2024). Dining etiquette. https://emilypost.com/advice/dining-etiquette [Covers the 4 o'clock utensil signal for "finished," napkin protocol, toasting, and excusing yourself from the table.]

34 von Drachenfels, S. (2000). The Art of the Table. Simon & Schuster. [The definitive illustrated reference on formal table setting, silverware, the BMW rule, and proper service — over 440 pages.

35 Tower, J. (2016). Table Manners: How to Behave in the Modern World and Why Bother. Farrar, Straus and Giroux. [A James Beard Award-winning chef's authoritative guide covering restaurant signals, check etiquette, hosting, and conversation rules.]

36 Post, L., & Senning, D. P. (2022). Emily Post's Etiquette: The Centennial Edition. Penguin Random House. [Covers all formal dining rules, napkin placement, utensil use, and restaurant behavior — the most cited etiquette authority in the United States.]

37 Assey, G. (2022). Dining Etiquette & Table Manners: Making Your Mark at Dining Experiences. Gerard Assey. [Step-by-step professional guide covering phone at the table, conversation rules, and professional dining conduct.]

38 Tower, J. (2016). Table Manners: How to Behave in the Modern World and Why Bother. Farrar, Straus and Giroux. [A James Beard Award-winning chef's authoritative guide covering restaurant signals, check etiquette, hosting, and conversation rules.]

39 The Emily Post Institute. (2024). Dining etiquette. https://emilypost.com/advice/dining-etiquette [Covers the 4 o'clock utensil signal for "finished," napkin protocol, toasting, and excusing yourself from the table.]

40 von Drachenfels, S. (2000). The Art of the Table. Simon & Schuster. [The definitive illustrated reference on formal table setting, silverware, the BMW rule, and proper service — over 440 pages.]

41 The Emily Post Institute. (2024). Dining etiquette. https://emilypost.com/advice/dining-etiquette [Covers the 4 o'clock utensil signal for "finished," napkin protocol, toasting, and excusing yourself from the table.]

42 Typology. (n.d.). *Differences: Eau de Cologne, Eau de Perfume, Eau de Toilette.* https://uk.typology.com/library/what-is-the-difference-between-eau-de-cologne-eau-de-toilette-eau-de-parfum-and-perfume

43 Yaws, C. L. (2015). *The Yaws handbook of vapor pressure: Antoine coefficients* (2nd ed.). Gulf Professional Publishing.

44 Herz, R. S. (2004). A naturalistic analysis of autobiographical memories triggered by olfactory visual and auditory stimuli. *Chemical Senses, 29*(3), 217–224. https://doi.org/10.1093/chemse/bjh025

REFERENCES

D FOR DANCE

[45] Graham,M. (1991). Blood memory: An autobiography. Doubleday

[46] De Mille, A. (1991). Dance to the piper. University of Minnesota press.

[47] Yen, K. A. (2025). The psychological effects of ballet and contemporary dance on female dancers: An embodiment perspective. *Communications in Humanities Research, 76*, 58–67. **https://doi.org/10.36690/chr.2025.26419**

[48] Su, K. (2024). The impact of dance on mental health: Exploring cognitive, emotional, self-esteem, and social interaction aspects. *International Journal of Education and Humanities, 15.* **https://doi.org/10.47363/IJEH/2024/15/1/23342**

[49] Conscientiousness and extraversion relate to responsiveness to tempo in dance. (2016). *Personality and Individual Differences, 101*, 1–6. https://doi.org/10.1016/j.paid.2016.05.019

[50] Cameron, D. J., Grahn, J. A., & Repp, B. H. (2022). Very low-frequency sound increases dance movement. *Current Biology, 32*(1), 1–7. https://doi.org/10.1016/j.cub.2021.11.014

[51] Cho, B. & O'Connor, P. (2024). Exploring the Interplay Between Religious Music, Emotions, and Ethics in Cultures Worldwide. Journal of Student Research 13(2), pp. 1-10. https://doi.org/10.47611/jsrhs.v13i2.6779

[52] Buxton, R. T., Pearson, A. L., Allou, C., Fristrup, K., & Wittemyer, G. (2021). A synthesis of health benefits of natural sounds and their distribution in national parks. *Proceedings of the National Academy of Sciences, 118*(14). **https://doi.org/10.1073/pnas.2013097118**

[53] Gautier, M. (2015). TEDx Talk: The connection between music and the human body. TEDx. https://www.ted.com/tedx

E FOR EDUCATION

[54] **Classy definition & meaning.** (n.d.). *Britannica Dictionary.* https://www.britannica.com/dictionary/classy

[55] **Growth mindset and enhanced learning.** (n.d.). *Stanford Teaching Commons.* https://teachingcommons.stanford.edu/teaching-guides/foundations-course-design/learning-activities/growth-mindset-and-enhanced-learning

[56] Informal learning. (2025). *Teachers Institute.* https://teachers.institute/learning-learner-development/incidental-learning-everyday-life/

[57] CNBC. (2016, November 30). *The 20 highest-paying jobs that don't require a bachelor's degree.* https://www.cnbc.com/2016/11/30/the-20-highest-paying-jobs-that-dont-require-a-bachelors-degree.html

[58]How does Rové Hair Salon stay ahead in the ever-changing hair trends. (2023). *Rové Hair Salon.* https://www.rovesalon.com/how-does-rove-hair-salon-stay-ahead-in-the-ever-changing-hair-trends/

[59] How has educational expansion shaped social mobility trends in the United States? (2015). *Demography, 52*(4), 1289–1309. https://doi.org/10.1007/s13524-015-0420-0

[60] Education. (2025). *Wikipedia.* https://en.wikipedia.org/wiki/Education

[61] Informal learning. (2025). *Wikipedia.* https://en.wikipedia.org/wiki/Informal_learning

[62] YouTube in education. (2023). *Wikipedia.* https://en.wikipedia.org/wiki/YouTube_in_education

[63]Challenges of misinformation in online learning: A post-pandemic perspective. (2025). *MDPI Encyclopedia, 5*(1). https://doi.org/10.3390/encyclopedia5010025

F FOR FASHION

[64]High-end fashion as a social phenomenon: Exploring the perceptions of designers and consumers. (2024). *Journal of Retailing and Consumer Services, 79.* https://doi.org/10.1016/j.jretconser.2024.103877

[65] The value of style. (2005). *Psychology Today.* https://www.psychologytoday.com/us/articles/200507/the-value-style

[66] These are the 10 timeless pieces every elegant woman over 50 should own. (2025). *Petite Dressing.* https://blog.petitedressing.com/these-are-the-10-timeless-pieces-every-elegant-woman-over-50-should-own/

[67] Getlatests. (2025). Mixing and Matching Patterns Like a Pro: A Fashion Inspiration Guide. Medium. https://getlatests.medium.com/mixing-and-matching-patterns-like-a-pro-a-fashion-inspiration-guide-e655f62eaeee

[68] The 8 best handbag colors that go with everything. (2018). *Who What Wear.* https://www.whowhatwear.com/best-handbag-colors

G FOR GLAMOUR

[69] Butcher, A. (2024). *The power of birthstones: Meaning, symbolism, and personal style.* International Gem Society. https://www.gemsociety.org

[70] Birthstone. (2025). https://en.wikipedia.org/wiki/Birthstone

I FOR INTERNATIONAL

[71] Haspelmath, M., & Tadmor, U. (2009). *Loanwords in the world's languages: A comparative handbook.* De Gruyter Mouton. https://cmc.marmot.org/EbscoAcademicCMC/ocn642692803

REFERENCES

72 Su, Q. (2025). Awakening the soul during travel: influence mechanism of memorable tourism experience on university students' life meaning. Frontiers in Psychology 16. https://doi.org/10.3389/fpsyg.2025.1521716

73 World Travel & Tourism Council. (2023). *The mental health and wellbeing benefits of travel.* Travel & Tourism Hub. https://travelhub.wttc.org/mental-health-and-wellbeing-benefits-of-travel

74 World's 9 most expensive foods: What makes them so pricey? (2025, January 14). *The Times of India.* https://timesofindia.indiatimes.com/life-style/food-news/worlds-9-most-expensive-foods-what-makes-them-so-pricey/photostory/122087130.cms

75 Wine-Searcher: The 2025 most expensive Chardonnays. (2025). *Wine-Intelligence.* https://wine-intelligence.com/blogs/wine-news-insights-wine-intelligence-trends-data-reports/wine-searcher-the-2025-most-expensive-chardonnays

J FOR JOURNAL

76 Beddow, K. (n.d.). *Journaling to preserve your memories.* Medium. https://katebeddow.medium.com/journaling-to-preserve-your-memories-fda774e4f548

77 Walsh, C. (2025). Kidlin's law | Casey Walsh. *LinkedIn.* https://www.linkedin.com/posts/casey-walsh-sug_kidlins-law-if-you-write-a-problem-down-activity-7282000132047306752-cDSg

78 Journaling for self-care and improvement. (2025). *Rutgers Learning Centers.* https://learningcenters.rutgers.edu/resources/journaling-self-care-and-improvement

79 Journaling for problem solving: Techniques for gaining clarity and insight. (2025). *JiYu – Journaling for self-reflection.* https://jiyushe.com/journaling-for-self-reflection/journaling-for-problem-solving-techniques-for-gaining-clarity-and-insight.html

80 Benefits of journaling. (n.d.). *Maat Journal.* https://www.maatjournal.com/benefits.html

81 Patricia. (2020). Creative journaling, part two: How journaling improves your memory. *Writing Your Life.* https://writingyourlife.org/journaling-improves-memory/

K FOR KNOWLEDGE

REFERENCES

[82] Cleopatra's education and intelligence. (2025). *Vocal Media.*
https://vocal.media/history/cleopatra-s-education-and-intelligence
[83] Queen Cleopatra: 8 reasons why she was such a powerful ruler. (2021). *Biography.com.* https://www.biography.com/royalty/a43842745/was-cleopatra-a-good-ruler
[84] Cleopatra's calculated gambles: A case study in strategic risk management. (2025). *University of Wasit.* https://educ.uowasit.edu.iq/archives/4292
[85] Book smart vs. street smart. (2007). *The Urban Review, 39*, 127–149. https://doi.org/10.1007/s11256-007-0050-0
[86] 부자들은 알고 당신은 모르는 성공법칙 5가지 (5 laws). (2025). *Tistory.* https://dictate2.tistory.com/1

L FOR LANGUAGE
[87] Nonverbal communication. (2025). *Wikipedia.* https://en.wikipedia.org/wiki/Nonverbal_communication
[88] Kulaeva, F., Khasueva, K., & Kulaev, A. (2025). Nonverbal communication in intercultural environment. *Journal of Intercultural Communication, 12*(3), 45–67. https://doi.org/10.5220/0001162500000333
[89] (Ethnologue. (n.d.). What are the top 200 most spoken languages? SIL International. Retrieved December 29, 2025, from https://www.ethnologue.com/)

M FOR MANNERS
[90] Is it ladylike to cross your legs? | Etiquette and posture. (2025). *Sivo.* https://blog.sivo.it.com/etiquette-and-posture/is-it-ladylike-to-cross-your-legs/

N FOR NAVIGATING
[91] Liberty name. (n.d.). *Wikipedia.* https://en.wikipedia.org/wiki/Liberty_name
[92] Stoner, J. L., Loken, B., & Blank, A. L. (2023). The name game: How naming products increases psychological ownership and subsequent consumer evaluations. *Journal of Consumer Psychology, 33*(3), 456–470. https://doi.org/10.1002/jcpy.1270

O FOR ORIGINAL

REFERENCES

93 Gino, F., Norton, M. I., & Ariely, D. (2010). The counterfeit self: The deceptive costs of faking it. *Psychological Science, 21*(5). https://doi.org/10.1177/0956797610366545

94 How to identify real gold: Easy tests for authenticity. (2025). *Expedite Africa*. https://www.expediteafrica.com/gold-market-updates/how-to-identify-real-gold/

95 How to verify the authenticity of 925 silver jewelry. (2025). *Fine Homes and Living*. https://www.finehomesandliving.com/fashion/how-to-verify-the-authenticity-of-925-silver-jewelry/article_7ec3ea2c-4295-4edd-9c71-7105767f8ef3.html

96 How to tell if a diamond is real without a tester?. (2022). *Diamond101*. https://diamond101.com/how-to-tell-if-a-diamond-is-real-without-a-tester/

97 How to identify a fake watch?. (2023). *Big Watch Buyers*. https://www.bigwatchbuyers.com/how-to-identify-a-fake-watch/

98 The ultimate guide to identifying and purchasing authentic designer bags online. (2025). *Alibaba.com*. https://www.alibaba.com/product-insights/the-ultimate-guide-to-identifying-and-purchasing-authentic-designer-bags-online.html

99 Satin material in luxury vs everyday fashion insights. (2025). *Szoneier Fabrics*. https://szoneierfabrics.com/satin-material-in-luxury-vs-everyday-fashion-segments/

100 Understanding leather grades: A complete guide for leather bags, shoes. (2025). *Carryfort*. https://carryfort.com/blogs/news/understanding-leather-grades-a-complete-guide-for-leather-bags-shoes-accessories

101 Polyester fabric: Properties, manufacturing, and uses. (2025). *Mekong Garment Vietnam*. https://mekonggarment.com/polyester-fabric-properties-manufacturing-and-uses/

102 Genuine leather products: Quality, grades & brand value. (2024). *Szoneier Leather*. https://szoneierleather.com/genuine-leather-products/

103 Bandura, A. (1977). *Social learning theory*. Prentice Hall.

Q FOR QUALITY

104 Chemicals that should disappear from cosmetics. (2013). *Environmental Working Group*. https://www.ewg.org/news-insights/news/chemicals-should-disappear-cosmetics

105 Cruelty-free brand directory. (2025). *Ethical Bunny*. https://www.ethicalbunny.com/brands/

106 Champagne. (2025, July 3). *Le Monde*. https://www.lemonde.fr/en/lifestyle/article/2025/07/04/champa

REFERENCES

---

gne-bubbles-with-excitement-for-10th-anniversary-of-its-unesco-designation_6743008_37.html

[107] Knowledge, attitude, and practices of restaurant and foodservice personnel in food allergy: A systematic review and meta-analysis. (2024). *Heliyon, 10*(13). https://doi.org/10.1016/j.heliyon.2024.e33431

[108] Do plastic water bottles leach plastic? (2025). *Environmental Literacy Council.* https://enviroliteracy.org/animals/do-plastic-water-bottles-leach-plastic/

[109] ENERGY STAR certified clothes washers. (2024). *EPA ENERGY STAR.* https://www.energystar.gov/most-efficient/me-certified-clothes-washers

S FOR SOCIALIZE

[110] Yoo, R. J. (2020). Finding true belonging in faith communities. *UMC.org.* https://www.umc.org/en/content/finding-true-belonging-in-faith-communities

[111] DYT. (2025). Personal branding: Establish a voice and tone for greater organic reach. *Medium.* https://doyourthng.medium.com/personal-branding-establish-a-voice-and-tone-for-greater-organic-reach-bd11ed3ce7a

[112] Okonkwo, I., & Awad, H. A. (2023). The role of social media in enhancing communication and collaboration in business. *Journal of Digital Marketing and Communication, 3*(1), 19–27. https://doi.org/10.53623/jdmc.v3i1.247

[113] The most expensive golf club memberships in the world. (2025, June 30). *Golf Monthly.* https://www.golfmonthly.com/features/the-most-expensive-golf-club-memberships-in-the-world

[114] Ivy League alumni networks. (2023). *Crimson Education.* https://www.crimsoneducation.org/us/blog/ivy-league-alumni-networks

[115] Ajrouch, K. J., Antonucci, T. C., & Janevich, M. R. (2017). Urbanism, neighborhood context, and social networks. *Journals of Gerontology: Social Sciences, 72*(8), 1245–1253. https://doi.org/10.1093/geronb/gbw124

[116] High net worth client acquisition strategist at Edward Jones. (2025). *Edward Jones.* https://careers.edwardjones.com/job/22625250/high-net-worth-client-acquisition-strategist-saint-louis-mo/

[117] Billionaire blockholders are stifling competition in corporate America. (2024, May 14). *ProMarket.* https://www.promarket.org/2024/05/15/billionaire-blockholders-are-stifling-competition-in-corporate-america/

[118] Dong, F., & Marquis, W. (2019). Social media use in the United States and its multifaceted effects on young adults: A 2019 cross-sectional study.

Journal of Strategic Innovation and Sustainability, 20(3). https://doi.org/10.33423/jsis.v20i3.7756

[119] Thompson, K. (2025). Personal branding on LinkedIn: Clarity, consistency, credibility. *LinkedIn.* https://www.linkedin.com/posts/kelliraethompson_your-professional-brand-essentially-people-activity-7364332766768885761—tZr

[120] Wells, R. (2024, January 8). Social media marketing skills in demand, worth $1.5 trillion by 2030. *Forbes.* https://www.forbes.com/sites/rachelwells/2024/01/09/social-media-marketing-skills-in-demand-worth-15-trillion-by-2030/

[121] The impact of social media on users' self-efficacy and loneliness: An analysis of the mediating mechanism of social support. (2024). *Psychology Research and Behavior Management, 17.* https://doi.org/10.2147/PRBM.S449079

[122] Key elements of a successful strategic event planning process. (2024). Event Management (EVM) Institute. https://evm.institute/event-planning/strategic-event-planning-success-elements/

U FOR USING THE RIGHT TOOL

[123] Can hot coffee break glass. (2021). *Iupilon.* https://iupilon.com/can-hot-coffee-break-glass/

[124] Hand tool ergonomics – job design. (2025). *Canadian Centre for Occupational Health and Safety.* https://www.ccohs.ca/oshanswers/ergonomics/handtools/jobdesign.html

[125] How often should you wash your sheets? (2025). *Sleep Foundation.* https://www.sleepfoundation.org/cleaning/how-often-should-you-wash-your-sheets

[126] Safe cooking tips. (2016). *American Society of Hand Therapists.* https://asht.org/sites/asht/files/docs/2016/Safe%20Cooking%20Tips%202016.pdf

[127] Microfiber: End users weigh in. (2025). *CleanLink.* https://www.cleanlink.com/sm/article/Microfiber-End-Users-Weigh-In—5064

[128] The art of formal table settings. (n.d.). *ASAP Linen.* https://www.asaplinen.com/the-art-of-linens-in-a-formal-table-setting/

[129] How to set a formal dinner table. (n.d.). *Martha Stewart.* https://www.marthastewart.com/945487/formal-table-setting

[130] Lopez, H. (n.d.). Rules of etiquette: How to fold napkin & rings [Video]. YouTube. https://www.youtube.com/watch?v=MpE9hQu7x8A

---

131 Setting the table. (2021). *University of Maryland Extension.*
https://extension.umd.edu/extension.umd.edu/sites/extension.umd.edu/files/2021-09/meal%20appeal%20setting%20the%20table.pdf

132 Handbag hygiene: How to prevent your handbag from spreading Covid-19. (2020, April 28). *Woman & Home.*
https://www.womanandhome.com/fashion/fashion-news/handbag-hygiene-353192/

133 Cultural differences on attention and perceived usability: Investigating color combinations of animated graphics. (2006). *International Journal of Human-Computer Studies, 64*(2), 103–122.
https://doi.org/10.1016/j.ijhcs.2005.06.003

134 (2024). Rose Color Meanings & Symbolism. ProFlowers.
https://www.proflowers.com/blog/rose-color-meanings

135 Attire guide: Dress codes from casual to white tie.wiki. *Emily Post Institute.* https://emilypost.com/advice/attire-guide-dress-codes-from-casual-to-white-tie

136 (2024). Gift-Giving: Reciprocal Exchange. Psychology Today.
https://www.psychologytoday.com/us/blog/your-money-and-your-brain/202402/gift-giving-reciprocal-exchange

137 (n.d.). Secrets To Successful Meetings. The Kamaron Institute.
https://kamaron.org/Successful-Meeting-Secrets

138 (2025). Five tips for giving culturally sensitive feedback. Harvard Business Review. https://hbr.org/2025/03/five-tips-for-giving-culturally-sensitive-feedback

139 (n.d.). The Role of Visual Aids in Presentations. Presentation Training Institute. https://www.presentationtraininginstitute.com/the-role-of-visual-aids-in-presentations/

140 (2013). Family Therapy Can Help: For People in Recovery From Mental Illness or Addiction. Substance Abuse and Mental Health Services Administration.
https://store.samhsa.gov/sites/default/files/d7/priv/sma13-4784.pdf

141 Brickwood, K., Watson, G., O'Brien, J. & Williams, A. D. (2019). Consumer-Based Wearable Activity Trackers Increase Physical Activity Participation: Systematic Review and Meta-Analysis. JMIR Mhealth and Uhealth. https://doi.org/10.2196/13794

142 Goyal, M., Singh, S., Sibinga, E. M. S., et al. (2014). Meditation programs for psychological stress and well-being: A systematic review and meta-analysis. JAMA Internal Medicine, 174(3), 357–368.
https://doi.org/10.1001/jamainternmed.2013.13018

143 Emmons, R. A., & McCullough, M. E. (2003). Counting blessings versus burdens: An experimental investigation of gratitude and subjective well-

being in daily life. Journal of Personality and Social Psychology, 84(2), 377–389. https://doi.org/10.1037/0022-3514.84.2.377
[144] Staff, M. C. (2024). First-aid kits: Stock supplies that can save lives. Mayo Clinic. https://www.mayoclinic.org/health/first-aid-kits/FA00067

V FOR VOLUNTEERING

[145] The value of volunteering. (2025). *Habitat for Humanity International.* https://www.habitat.org/sites/default/files/documents/Value-of-Volunteering-EvidenceBrief.pdf
[146] Pranke, D. (2025). How strategic volunteering can positively impact your career. *Career Development Services.* https://careerservices.fgcu.edu/blog/2025/07/07/how-strategic-volunteering-can-positively-impact-your-career/
[147] 5 benefits of community service. (2024). *Public Relations Society of America.* https://www.prsa.org/docs/default-source/prssa-docs/chapter-firm-resources/community-service-fact-card-for-prssa-faculty-advisers.pdf?sfvrsn=6d2e4a70_0
[148] The Holy Bible, New International Version. Biblica, 2011. Deuteronomy 15:10. https://www.bible.com/bible/111/DEU.15.10.NIV
[149] Deloitte survey: Workplace volunteer opportunities can unlock a greater sense of connection and a more positive work experience for employees. (2024, June 3). *Deloitte US.* https://www2.deloitte.com/us/en/pages/about-deloitte/articles/press-releases/deloitte-purpose-survey-volunteerism.html
[150] El-Amin, A. (2022). Utilizing effective volunteer management to elevate nonprofit organizational capacity. *Journal of Nonprofit Education and Leadership, 12*(1), 1–15. https://doi.org/10.18666/JNEL-2022-11716
[151] Charitable contributions. (2025). *Internal Revenue Service.* https://www.irs.gov/charities-non-profits/charitable-contributions
[152] Employer matching gifts. (n.d.). *Habitat for Humanity.* https://www.habitat.org/support/workplace-giving/matching-gifts

W FOR WEALTHY

[153] Koenig, H. G., McCullough, M. E., & Larson, D. B. (2001). Handbook *of religion and health.* Oxford University Press. https://www.oup.com/us/catalog/general/subject/?view=usa&view=usa&ci=9780195118667&cp=24297

REFERENCES

154 Carl Jung Depth Psychology. (2020, July 21). *Carl Jung: Where your fear is, there is your task!!!*
https://carljungdepthpsychologysite.blog/2020/07/21/fear-is-there-is-your/
155 Carl Jung: How fear reveals your true purpose. (2025, January 24). *Whispering Ideas* [Video]. YouTube.
https://www.youtube.com/watch?v=4F-a2C0hiUY
156 Cannon, D. (n.d.). Nothing is impossible: Create anything you want [Lecture]. Scribd. https://www.scribd.com/document/881885266/Dolores-Cannon-Nothing-is-Impossible-Create-Anything-YouWant-Meditation-Visualization
157 Etiquette classes for ladies in London & online | Emma Dupont Etiquette School. (2025). *Emma Dupont Etiquette School*
https://emmadupontetiquetteschool.co.uk/

X FOR XOXO
158 Unconditional love: What it is and how to find it. (2016). *Healthline.*
https://www.healthline.com/health/relationships/unconditional-love
159 Daily communication, conflict resolution, and marital quality in Chinese marriage: A three-wave, cross-lagged analysis. (2018). *Journal of Family Psychology, 32*(3), 366–375. https://doi.org/10.1037/fam0000390
160 Kramer, J. (2024). Unconditional love vs. lack of boundaries: Understanding the difference. *Counseling in Bethesda.*
https://counselinginbethesda.com/2024/08/21/unconditional-love-vs-lack-of-boundaries-understanding-the-difference/
161 Hesse, H. (n.d.). *Some of us think holding on makes us strong.* BrainyQuote.
https://www.brainyquote.com/quotes/hermann_hesse_384604
162 Actions speak louder than words. (2024). *The Good Energy Daily.*
https://thegoodenergydaily.beehiiv.com/p/actions-words-power-love-trust-apologies
163 Matchmaking vs. dating apps. Which one is right for me? (2025). *Tawkify.* https://tawkify.com/blog/from-the-experts/matchmaking-vs-dating-apps-which-one-is-right-for-me
164 Matching hypothesis. (n.d.). *Wikipedia.*
https://en.wikipedia.org/wiki/Matching_hypothesis
165 Committing to a romantic partner: Does attractiveness matter? A dyadic approach. (2021). *Personality and Individual Differences, 176,* 110765. https://doi.org/10.1016/j.paid.2021.11076

REFERENCES

Y FOR YOUTHFUL

[166] Vogels, E. A. (2019, September 8). Millennials stand out for their technology use. *Pew Research Center.* https://www.pewresearch.org/fact-tank/2019/09/09/us-generations-technology-use/

[167] Henry Ford quotes. (n.d.). *Henry Ford Quotes.* https://www.henry-ford.net/english/quotes.html

[168] We don't stop playing because we grow old; we grow old because we stop playing. (n.d.). *Inspiring Quotes.* https://inspiringquotes.com/quotes-to-help-you-stay-young-and-spry-forever/

Z FOR ZONE

[169] The Fact Site. (2025). Twenty-six facts about the number 26. https://www.thefactsite.com/number-twenty-six-facts/

[170] *Paul Ekman Group.* Universal emotions. (n.d.). https://www.paulekman.com/resources/universal-emotions/

[171] Sagui-Henson, S., Smith, J. A., & Lee, R. (2022). How emotions guide decision-making: Insights for well-being. Therapy Hub. https://www.therapyhub.com/articles/how-emotions-guide-decisions

[172] Csikszentmihalyi, M. (1990). Flow: The Psychology of Optimal Experience. Harper & Row.

[173] Merriam-Webster. (2025). Calendar week. In Merriam-Webster.com dictionary. https://www.merriam-webster.com

[174] Britannica. (2025). Latin alphabet. Encyclopaedia Britannica. https://www.britannica.com/topic/Latin-alphabet

[175] Britannica. (2025). Number symbolism. Encyclopaedia Britannica. https://www.britannica.com/topic/number-symbolis

[176] Wikipedia. (2025). 26 (number). https://en.wikipedia.org/wiki/26_(number)

[177] Gray, H. (2000). Gray's Anatomy: The Anatomical Basis of Clinical Practice (39th ed.). Churchill Livingstone

[178] Williams, P. L. (Ed.). (1989). Gray's Anatomy (37th ed.). Churchill Livingstone.

[179] Royal Society of Chemistry. (2025). Iron — element 26. https://www.rsc.org/periodic-table/element/26/iron

[180] Wikipedia. (2025). Tetragrammaton. https://en.wikipedia.org/wiki/Tetragrammaton

[181] Charisma Magazine. (2026, January 2). Supernatural significance of 2026: The prophetic meaning behind 26. https://mycharisma.com

---

[182] Charisma Magazine. (2026, January 2). Supernatural significance of 2026: The prophetic meaning behind 26. https://mycharisma.com

[183] Pratt, J. P. (2004). The AD 26 view of the fifteenth year of Tiberius. Academia.edu. https://www.academia.edu/44668230

[184] Wikipedia. (2025). Bosonic string theory. https://en.wikipedia.org/wiki/Bosonic_string_theory

[185] Wikipedia. (2025). 26 (number). https://en.wikipedia.org/wiki/26_(number)

[186] Wikipedia. (2025). List of Academy Awards for Walt Disney. https://en.wikipedia.org/wiki/List_of_Academy_Awards_for_Walt_Disney

[187] cube20.org. (2014). God's Number is 26 in the quarter turn metric. https://www.cube20.org/qtm/

[188] National Archives. (2025). 26th Amendment to the United States Constitution. https://www.archives.gov

[189] Council on Foreign Relations. (2025, December 2). Ten anniversaries to note in 2026. https://www.cfr.org/articles/ten-anniversaries-note-2026

[190] Littler Mendelson. (2025). Employers who pay biweekly may have 27 paydays in 2026 — are you ready? https://www.littler.com/news-analysis/asap/employers-pay-biweekly-may-have-27-paydays-2026-are-you-ready

[191] ScienceDirect. (2024). Chromosome number — an overview. https://www.sciencedirect.com/topics/agricultural-and-biological-sciences/chromosome-number

[192] Science.gov. (2024). Cytogenetic features of antlions (Myrmeleontidae). https://www.science.gov/topicpages/c/chromosome+number+2n.html

[193] Karma & Tide. (2025). Number 8 symbolism: Spiritual meaning, prosperity, and the infinity connection. https://karmaandtide.com/numerology/basic-numbers/number-8-symbolism-spiritual-prosperity-infinity

[194] Warriors Divine. (2024). Lucky number 8: Discover how lucky number 8 brings prosperity and abundance. https://warriorsdivine.com/blogs/the-path/lucky-number-8-discover-how-lucky-number-8-brings-prosperity-and-abundance